SPECIAL UNITS

MARINES

Illustrations: Octavio Díez Cámara, Audiovisuele Dienst Kon. Marine, GIAT Industries, Santiago García Gaya and Antonio Ros Pau.

Production: Ediciones Lema, S.L.
Editorial Director: Josep M. Parramón Homs
Text: Octavio Díez Cámara
Editor: Eva Mª Durán
Coordinator: Eduardo Hernández
Layout: Rakel Medina

ISBN 84-95323-40-0

Fotochromes and phototypesetting: Novasis, S.A.
Barcelona (Spain)
Printed in Spain

MARINES

UNITED STATES MARINE CORPS

The US maintains a military policy that supports the global presence of the diverse elements of its armed forces. One of its components is the Marine Corps or the United States Marine Corps (USMC), a force with the capacity for action anywhere in the world thanks to the troops, resources and aircraft that are constantly afloat aboard vessels of the Navy. In addition to its great capacity as a combat element that can rapidly be deployed to where its presence is required, its members enjoy, in addition, great prestige both in and out of their own country deriving from constant collaboration with similar forces from other countries.

Tradition and modernity

The origins of the USMC date back to 1741 when England recruited 3000 colonists in order to form Gooch's Marine contingent that attacked the Spanish town of Cartagena. Since then its troops have been involved in all kinds of battles among which one can indicate the military actions in Liberia in 1843, the 1900

Transport

The decks, the holds and the floodable docks of the amphibious assault vessels of the marine are used to give mobility to the expeditionary forces of the marines, it being quite usual to have vessels sailing constantly in order to intervene wherever necessary.

Multi-mission

The American Marines are an army with capacity for deployment anywhere in the world and ready to carry out the most varied of missions. Of outstanding note is its capacity to undertake all types of combat activity and pacification.

combats in China on the occasion of the rebellion of the Boxers, its participation in the battles of Iwo Jima and Okinawa during the Second World War, its actions against the Vietcong during the Vietnam war, its deployment as a pacifying element in Lebanon, the actions against Iraq during Operation Desert Shield in 1991 or its labor in the evacuations from Albania in 1997.

Large potential for combat.

In order to project its global deployment capacity, a force of 170,000 troops has been authorized, to which 40,000 more men that constitute the reserve must be added. This last group may be enlarged to 100,000 in a relatively short period of time.

With a cost of 6 % of the US Defense Department budget, the USMC is capable of maintaining active 12 % of its troops, 23 % of ground troops and 14 % of its tactical airplanes. To carry out support tasks some 18,000 civilians are required. Its current organization comprises the Joint

General Headquarters (SJTF HQ, Standing Joint Task Force Headquarters) at Camp Lejeune in North Carolina, in the 1st Marine amphibious Command located at Camp Pendelton in California, a second based at Camp Lejeune and Quantico, a third in the Japanese base of Camp Butler at Okinawa and a fourth as reserve in the city of New Orleans, in the State of Louisiana. A force of which 23 % is deployed in times of peace externally to the home bases

The 1st Command that forms part of the RDJTF, Rapid Deployment Joint Task Force, comprises the 1st Marine Division of Camp Pendelton and the 3rd Aviation Wing in Nevada; the second integrates the 2nd Division of Camp Lejeune and the 2nd Wing distributed between the bases of Camps Cherry Point and New River (both in North Carolina). The third is formed by 3rd Division Camp Butler and the 1st Wing of Futema, whilst the fourth Division and the fourth Wing is made up of the reserve forces (MARFORRES, Marine Forces Rerserve) that are distributed in over 191 different locations. To the former we must add the battalions associated with security tasks in the General Headquarters of the Atlantic and the Pacific and an independent brigade that acts in Hawaii with the support of the Air Station at Kaneone Bay.

Each of the divisions include some 18,000 persons that make up three Infantry Regiments, one Artillery, logistic backup and battalion combat tanks, armored amphibious assault, armored reconnaissance and engineers.

Operational organization

The operative elements of the USMC are distributed between the marine Forces of the Atlantic under the command of COMMARFORLANT, those of the Pacific controlled under COMMARFORPAC, and the forces and security battalions.

The first two provide all the combat elements that supply the Task Groups Air-Ground (MAGTS's) with elements of terrestrial, aerial and support control. One finds various MAGTF's in relation to their size: MEF, Marine Expeditionary Force, with a combat autonomy of 60 days, MEU, Marine Expeditionary Unit, with capacity for 15 days, and SPMAGTF, Special Purpose MAGTF, that can operate as long as necessary, since it is organized to suit specific contingencies.

At present there are three MEF´s formed, of which one is located at bases in Arizona and California , the second is based in North and South Carolina, and the third is spread over Japanese cities in Okinawa and Mainland. Crews are partly located aboard vessels that are either constantly at sea or based at port. There are also various complementary warehouses strategically distributed around the world considered pre-positioned forces (MPF).

It should be pointed out that the USM is composed of little more than 2000 people organized as elements for imme-

BROWNING HEAVY MACHINE GUN M2HB

This heavy machine gun originally built in 1923 for aerial use, was designated M2 in 1933. Since then it has become an indispensable element for combat, for which various mounts have been designed that range from the tripod that the infantry use to turrets to equip the most varied of vehicles.
The M2 manufactured in the US by various companies, are used by the marines to support movements, it being usual for them to be mobilized by means of a mount on the HUMMER vehicle, or for them to be carried by the infantry in their advance.

One of its most significant characteristics is that it fires caliber 12.70 x 99 cartridges (.50 Browning) at a rate of 600 rounds a minute with an effective range of 0,9 miles with a barrel of 1.143 m that can be quickly changed and that is noted for its high accuracy, and it weighs about 38 Kgs.
Easy to aim, simple to use, very robust and with very few logistical requirements this firearm will continue to be a reference to distinguish a successful design that does not comply with all the expectations of the military.

deployed in the Mediterranean and another in the West Pacific and if the situation so demands, they may be supported by another in the Atlantic or in the Indian Ocean with capacity to provide up to four large amphibian assault vessels.

The USM battalion is organized to carry out assault attacks, it receives the denomination BLT (Battalion Landing Team) and supports itself with other elements such as artillery, amphibian assault vehicles, combat tanks and recognition armors. The marines are distributed between the General Headquarters and the companies Alfa, Beta and Charlie, including in this latter elements ready to operate in special reconnoitering. This configuration allows the MEU to carry out, in addition to the general missions of the Marine Corps, operations such as combat in urban areas, tactical recovery of personnel or destroyed apparatus (TRAP, Tactical Recovery Aircraft and Personal), surveillance and stealth reconnaissance, attacks on oil and gas platforms and rescue of hostages in extreme conditions.

diate action of limited scope. For some time now, they have possessed special qualifications for carrying out special missions (SOC, Special Operations Capable). They have their own logistic support that allows them to carry out combat actions for 15 days. In addition, they are under the command of a Colonel and have the status of a battalion, reinforced with helicopters and fighter bombers (ACE, Air Combat Element) and a support and service group (MSSG, USM Service Support Element). Usually there is a USM

Man
The most important part of the USCM are its members, for which reason special care is taken when recruiting and training. As a result the units have great potential for use in an wide range of activities.

The security forces (MCSF Marine Corps Security Forces) depend directly on the Chief of Naval Operations (CNO) and have more than 3,500 men to carry out the vigilance of naval bases and installations and configure detachments to certain vessels. The security battalion (MSGB Marine Security Guard Battalion) has its members spread out over 121 diplomatic delegations throughout 115 countries.

The best and most varied equipment

The particular amphibious activities assigned to the USMC imply the use of special equipment that allows for the carrying out of a great variety of missions.

This equipment includes elements for terrestrial combat as well as various types

Combat
The marine has been instructed to become the driving force of amphibious assaults. Moreover, his training permits him to operate also in wooded areas, deserts and mountains.

Armoring

The LAV 25 is a type of armored vehicle of United States origin that is noted for its undercarriage with 8 driving wheels, a great transport capacity in its armored interior, and for its armored turret with a rapid firing 25 mm gun.

of aircraft that act as support to movements and provide a high capacity of fire.

To these must be added the vessels of the American navy that provide strategic mobility permitting rapid deployment to anywhere in the world.

The resources for terrestrial combat

Personal equipment, armament and fire support elements make up the varied array of material used by the US Marines. The first group includes: a standard uniform BDU (Battle Dress Uniform), protective equipment of PASGT system, communication equipment, ICB boots of Belleville Shoe Manufacturing, rucksacks, tents, LBV jackets (Load Bearing Vest), NBQ war uniforms (Nuclear, Bacteriologic and Chemical) or night vision goggles AN/PVS-5 & 7 this one with a third generation caption tube.

All weather

The new AV-8B Harrier fighter bomber is noted for its powerful engine, for incorporating a radar in the nose that allows it to aim at any target and to guide various types of missiles, it also has a cabin compatible with the use of night vision goggles.

The individual equipment includes: M1911 Colt pistols caliber .45 ACP and Beretta M-92 9x19 mm Parabellum; Revolvers caliber .38 Special, Colt Assault rifles M4 & M16A2 firing ammunition caliber .223 Remington in magazines for 30 cartridges, sub-rifles MP5N 9 Parabellum, shotguns caliber 12/70 inclu-

Nashville
This is the name of the LPD-13 that came into service in February 1970 and that is noted for its capacity to transport men, vehicles and helicopters, both in its interior and its helicopter platform on deck and can carry up to 17.000 tons.

ding Mossberg Mariner M590, light machine guns M240 SAW 5.56x45 mm, grenade launchers M203 40 mm that can be fitted to the assault rifles, rifles M14 and precision rifles M40A1 with breech block for .308 Winchester and anti-material rifles Barrett M-82 that fire 12.70x99 or .50 Browning cartridges.

In the group of support firearms there are: rocket launchers AT-4 & B 300 SMAW, light machine guns M60E3 and M-240G, heavy machine guns M2, anti-tank missile launchers Javelin, that are progressively replacing the DRAGON and TOW, automatic grenade launchers Sako MK-19 mod. 4, light mortars M-224 60 mm and medium M-252 81.

As collective armaments are found Stinger anti-aircraft missiles, towed howitzers M101A1 of 105 mm and M198

of 155, M1A1 Abrams combat tanks provided with 120 mm guns, self propelled howitzers M109A3 of 155 mm and M-110A2 of 203, MLRS multiple launch rocket systems, Hercules recovery vehicles M88A1E1 and scissor bridge launchers M60A1 AVBL, wheeled vehicles 6x6 LVA (Light Armored Vehicle) in different versions and amphibious assault vehicles type AAV-7A1 in its different versions for transportation of personnel, recovery and command that have been based on the model LVTP7.

For all types of transport some 17,000 HUMMER (High wheeled Multipurpose wheeled vehicles) are used, some Jeeps M-151, 5 ton lorries M969 and heavy Oshkosh lorries Mk48 VLS (Vehicle Landing System) that serve to provide mobility to diverse units that range from mobile fuel deposits to shelters prepared

Pilot
The pilot wings and the emblems of firearms and rifles can be seen on the jacket of the marine. He wears the working uniform of the staff of the aviation wing that are not involved in combat operations.

to receive specific installations. They also benefit from various types of towing vehicles of various sizes and configurations.

Aerial and naval supports

The first are grouped in the MAGTF and comprise four Aviation Wings spread out over air bases (MCAS, Marine Corps Air Stations) and are also loaded onto ships, the former being the 1st (MAW

Marine Aircraft Wing) based at Iwaki and Futema in Japan. The second is based at Cherry Point and New River in North Carolina and Beaufort in South Carolina. The third is spread over Yuma in Arizona Camp Pendelton and Miramar in California with the fourth as MAW Reserve.

Amongst the above are some 200 bomber fighters F/A-18 Hornet, 20 electronic war apparatus EA-6B Prowler, 150 fighter-bomber AV-8B Harrier II and AB-8B that is in the process of being transformed to variant II (that includes all-weather radar) 50 KC-130 Hercules for the aerial re-fuelling of aircraft, nearly 200 Super-Cobra attack helicopters AH-1W and about a dozen Huey utility helicopters UH-1N that are currently being modernized to keep them in active service for another 20 years, 250 SEA-Knight medium transport helicopters CH-46E, and 150 Stallion CH-53D and E Super Stallion heavy transport helicopters. The medium transport helicopters will be replaced by V-22 Osprey of which the first units have been in the process of being received at the USS Tortuga, since the beginning of 1999, for operational evaluation (OPEVAL).

The MAWs also form anti-aircraft defense groups: short range missile launchers FIM-92 Stingers, Avenger mobile systems that combine four of the latter with heavy machine guns, and medium

Vehicle
The HUMMER is a very mobile all terrain vehicle that is noted for its four-wheel-drive system, its powerful engine and for incorporating a system that allows the inflation of the tires from inside to facilitate its circulation on all kinds of terrain.

Anti-aircraft
The Stinger is a short-range anti-aircraft defense system composed of a launch tube that may be managed by a single man, whilst a companion watches out for the arrival of possible targets and takes care of communications.

range Hawk launchers, forming a collection of weapon that combines very mobile elements with others of area defense.

Amongst the naval resources assigned for transfer and supplied by the navy, there are eleven Austis LPD (Landing platform Dock) that displace 17,000 tons. Six Wasp LHD (Landing Helicopter Dock) that will be complemented with a more apt vessel in 2001; five Tarawa LHA (Landing Helicopter Attack), twelve LSD (Landing Ship Dock) type Whidbey Island and Harpers Ferry and two Newport class LST (Landing Ship Tank), anticipating the acquisition of LSD San Antonio from 2002. In the docks of the above mentioned, LCAC (Landing Craft Air Cushion) are usually transported, allowing rapid movements of men and material towards the beachhead

Sea Dragon
This is the name given to the program that anticipates the needs that the Corps will have over the next few years, previsions that are completed with the requirement of the Chiefs of the General Staff and reflected in "The Joint Vision (JV) 2010"

In order to improve the effectiveness of the powerful USCM military organization, work is being carried out in several areas. The first is dedicated to the combatant who will find his training enriched by the BWT program (Basic War Training) and MCT (Marine Combat

ATTACK HELICOPTERS AH-1 COBRA

The Marines have been a good customer for the American company Bell, from whom it has been buying different models of the attack helicopter Cobra, vehicles that have been updated to the most modern standards. At the moment the USCM uses a considerable number of AH-1W Super Cobra that are noted for having two higher powered General Electric turbines, thus improving the agility of the helicopter, also incorporating semi-wings of greater resistance permitting the firing of AGM-65 Maverik missiles or AIM Sidewinder; included is a two-seater cabin that has new display screens; and a new main rotor that incorporates new blades manufactured with very advanced materials to improve resistance to impacts.

The features of this helicopter, that measures 17.68 m and can raise itself with a maximum weight of 6,690 kg, include a flying speed of 278 Km/h, an autonomy of 587 Km without having to recur to add-on tanks, a service ceiling of 4,200 m and a load capacity of 1 ton of weapons and 946 Kg of fuel.
In order to maintain its potential over next two decades they will be improved with the H-1. Said measure consists of a new rotor with four blades, a sophisticated pilot cabin, revised transmission and structural modifications in order to support half wings with 6 anchorage points, and other details that configure it into BW Configuration that stands out for its superior agility, greater speed and greater loading capacity.

Training) the final exam including a two and a half day tactical exercise. His equipment is also improved with several elements: specially designed combat clothing resulting from the application of the ICCE program (Individual Combat Clothing and Equipment) and MEP (Marine Enhancement Program) that includes from leather boots and laces to bulletproof jackets; chemical and biological detection elements such as the

JCAD (Joint Chemical Agent Detector) or the SUBD (Small Unit Biological Detector); protection systems such as the AGLEP goggles (Advanced Ground Laser Eye Protection) that protect the eyes from laser beams in the battlefield, and more lethal weapon systems that employ sophisticated scopes that facilitate targeting and integrate reception and sending of information in real time. The facility for combat is complemented with

new very short and long-range missiles that will replace various models in current use; light 155/32 mm howitzers such as the British LTH (Light Towed Howitzer) that is already being evaluated; tracked armored amphibious assault vehicles type AAAV (Advanced Amphibious Assault Vehicle) of which the first prototypes designed by General Dynamics Amphibious Systems are already being evaluated; engineer combat vehicles such as the

CBV Grizzly (Combat Beacher Vehicle) that is based on the M1A1 platform and thermal cameras type AVDTV in order to improve the driving characteristics of armored vehicles and tanks.

Communications will be implemented with C4I command, control and intelligence systems, tactical mobile terminals TCO, IAS valises for analysis of intelligence or lightweight radios type SINC-GARS (Ground Airborne Radio System) for agile change of frequency. As for vehicles, the construction of the HUMMER at a rate of 1,750 per year is notable, as also is the modernization of lorries M969 to increase its all-terrain load to 7 tons and the revision of the MK48 VLS lorries. The incorporation of different robots and remote controlled aircraft are also planned for use in the collection of information and reconnaissance in dangerous areas such as cities or anti-aircraft batteries.

As a complement to equipment a variation of the process of incorporation of men has been programmed in order to improve their aptitude and increase their capacity to use the more and more sophisticated armament systems.

Training
During a parade at the San Diego base (California) a group of marines can be seen carrying, in a martial manner, the banner of the Corps and the unit to which they belong.

THE AMERICAN RECON

The infantry of the US Marine (USCM United States Marine Corps) includes among its principal combat elements diverse units assigned to special actions both in the vanguard of amphibious troop movements as in those actions where a better qualified personnel are needed. These special groups receive the denomination of Recon in memory of the reconnaissance activities carried out during the beginning of its formation.

Parachutists and Marines

The need for more specialized troops than those that fought in the general fronts during WWII, led the USCM to train specialized units. In January 1942 special training was carried out in which two officers and twenty 1st division marines took part in what led to the creation of a reconnaissance group. It was the first marine unit in history to be organized and trained for reconnaissance activities.

Notable success

Its first commanding officer was Captain James Logan Jones who gave the unit

Rifles

The Recon have available to them a large collection of weapons, including the German rifle MP5 of Heckler und Köck. The one in the photograph corresponds to a training model that permits marksmen to maintain their level of qualification.

such an impulse that a year later a total of 98 men formed part of the Amphibious Recon Company.

Some of those men were later deployed aboard the submarine Nautilus and carried out reconnaissance activities on the island of Apamama. Later they carried out other activities in Guadalcanal and Bougainville on the Island of Salomon. At the same time, in 1942, the USCM Raider Battalion was created, its task being to carry out rapid and punctual actions such as those carried out by the British Royal Marine Commandos, later other battalions were formed until they constituted a regiment that was dissolved when the fighting stopped.

Lightweight

The missions assigned to the Recon require them to be self-sufficient in the area where they are deployed. They therefore carry lightweight equipment that allows them to combat and survive as long as the mission lasts.

Destruction

A Recon team can be divided into two halves in order to face a potentially strong enemy. In this case they make use of the B-300 rocket-launcher, the 40 mm grenade-launcher and assault rifles M16A2 and M4.

During the Korean war, reconnaissance missions were also carried out, such as the one led by Captain Houghton that penetrated 70 Kms into North Korea. It was usual for these troops to work together with the marine combat divers. The First Amphibious Recon Platoon was set up in March 1951 and within two years it reached the grade of a company and in 1954 became a Battalion.

With these troops, it was possible to first form a company directly dependent on the Atlantic fleet and another on that of the Pacific, completing the conversion in 1957 from the 1st Amphibious Reconnaissance Company to the 1st Force Reconnaissance Company, element which was deployed in Vietnam in October 1965. The specific needs of this conflict, in which it was common for the patrols to carry out vigilance in the deeply dense forests seeking the enemy that rejected

Helicopter transport

The heavy Chinook Helicopters CH-47 of the US navy are sometimes used to transport the Recon Platoons to the deployment area, nevertheless it is more normal for them to use the many types of helicopters that belong to the Marine Corps.

any contact, led to the creation of two other reconnaissance companies that participated actively in the Asian conflict until 1975.

The 80s and 90s

From that moment onwards, in order to create elements to carry out the most varied of naval missions, a greater specialization of members was undertaken. Its participation in missions such as the invasion of the Island

of Grenada with reconnaissance missions carried out by the 2nd Recon Battalion, is well known as are the actions against Iran in 87 and 88 in which they occupied one of the oil platforms in the Persian Gulf. Another outstanding event were the rescue of two pilots who ejected themselves from a fighter plane F-111 during a raid on Libya and the actions carried out during the Desert Storm operation, which included the special missions for localization and destruction of deciphering equipment on Iraqi territory, or the occupation of the American Embassy in Kuwait during the re-conquest of the city.

More recent are the actions in Liberia for which the curious decision was made to only carry Colt semi-automatic weapons M1911 caliber .45 ACP and one M-16 machine gun per team. They also captured General Aideed during their intervention in Somalia, but which they later abandoned after a few months because the US armed forces were not able to convince the confronting parties to sign a cease-fire agreement. They were also involved in the rescue of pilot O'Grady who ejected himself from a fighter bomber F-16 on Yugoslav territory during that crisis.

Recently, there has been much talk finally about possible dissolution, but it has been decided to maintain a Recon Battalion and a Force Recon Company in each of the active divisions. The first are formed by a reduced group of specialized personnel in tactical reconnaissance. The second are formed by a unit commanded by a Lieutenant-Colonel who at the same time groups four

PRECISION RIFLE M40A1

In 1966, the USCM adopted the Remington M700 commercial rifle as a precision rifle to which it assigned the denomination M40. Of its particular merits may be mentioned its soft manual lock, that follows the Mauser principle and its good firing characteristics derived from the use of 7.62x51 mm cartridges (.308 Winchester). Used by the Marines in Vietnam they soon saw the need to improve its ergonomic characteristics, so the manufacturer, the Remington Arms company of Llion in New York was asked to prepare a new improved model.
Thus in 1976 the M40A1 model was created that combi-

nes the previous weapon with a large 24 inch barrel. In stainless steel and chromed black externally in order to prevent corrosion, it has an ergonomic fiberglass butt manufactured by McMillan in its Phoenix plant. In addition it is camouflaged externally for mimetism and a sharp Unertl optical scope of 10x magnification and a Mil-Dot reticule which was first fitted in 1980.
The basic characteristics are: 6.57 Kg magazine for 5 cartridges, 1.117 mts length, maximum target range 900 meters and 1/2 Minute of Angle (MOA) precision using Match Lake City M118 ammunition.

Recon Platoon commanded by lieutenants and three Direct Action Platoons controlled by Captains. Each one of the seven above mentioned are formed by sixteen Marines grouped into patrols of four members each.

Their activity is to make up the eyes and ears of the Division as reaction elements confronted by specific situations. Those that demand the use of men specialized in aerial infiltrations of High Altitude such as High Altitude Low Opening (HALO) and High Altitude High Opening (HAHO), under-

Recon
The three active divisions of the USMC incorporate the Recon, special action troops assigned special reconnaissance actions both in the vanguard of amphibious movements as in other military actions.

water missions or specific attacks on the most varied of objectives.

The lengthy selection process
The assigned missions of Recon include: obtaining information from the enemy, neutralizing specific elements of the enemy, disseminating all kinds of sensors, capturing previously selected prisoners, carrying out special reconnaissance of terrain or guiding precision munitions in their terminal phase.

Specific preparation
The Recon marines as they are known in the military environment, are considered the elite of the Marines. To be recruited they are required to have previous experience in the Corps of at least 3-4 years and have participated in some kind of course such as the SSP (Scout Sniper Platoon) for selected marksmen, or to have participated in a significant activity such as having served in the security of diplomatic delegations.

The personnel who aspire to integrate into these units must overcome the "Army Airborne Test" that is required for aero-transported troops . This exam includes running 3 miles in less than 18 minutes, overcoming obstacles in less than 5 minutes, swiming 500 m, retrieving a heavy object from the bottom of a swimming-pool and other activities that allow for the selection of the most physically prepared. Following an interview with the leader of the Company that evaluates them psychologically, they then go on to form part of the RIP (Recon Indoctrination Platoon) where they complete their training.

They will later study at the School of Amphibious Reconnaissance in Little Creek or Coronado where they will have to

pass the three week diving course, then practice the automatic parachute jump for a month at Fort Benning and afterwards on to the Infantry School, it being quite common, that out of 60 that present themselves only 2 or 3 are finally selected. This formation will be completed at their posting where they will perfect training in different areas. They will pass specific training such as the SERE (Survival, Escape, Evasion and Reconnaissance School) that combines teaching in areas such as survival or withdrawing from filtration. The SSS (Scout Sniper School) perfects their training as marksmen and the JEST (Jungle Environment Survival Training) prepares them to work in jungle areas. The better prepared may be selected to be integrated into Team 6 of the Sea, Air and Land or the Delta Force, both being very specialized anti terrorist units managed respectively by the Marine and the Army.

Infiltration
Where great autonomy and a high capacity of fire is needed, use is made of all terrain vehicles M151 that have been modified with overturning bars and mounts for supporting several weapons.

SPANISH MARINE INFANTRY BRIGADE

Spain has a long amphibian tradition and possesses on the oldest Marine Infantry (IM) in the world. This is made up of independent groups and several divisions, one of them being the Armada (TEAR) that has its base at the San Fernando garrison in Cádiz with a resolute and prepared force, The Infantry Marine Brigade (BRIMAR), figuring amongst its elements.

Created in 1537

During the nearly five centuries that the troops of the Armada have been in active service, there have been several configurations that have allowed its adaptation to the most varied military demands both operational and tactical. During this period they have demonstrated their high value as an element of intervention, capable of combat in very different scenarios.

A long historical process.

The first reference that we have of the Marine Troops dates back to 1248, when King Fernando II organized a navy to conquer Seville. Three decades later, it would be Charles I who would create the "Compañías Viejas del Mar de Nápoles" that made up the infantry troops who embarked in galleys. This is the first clear evidence of the formation of the IM.

Charles I organized the first battle action when he grouped 36,000 men to fight against the Pirate Barbarrouse . These acts were followed by others such as the squadron that fought the Turks in 1565, leading to the creation in 1566 of the Galleys of Sicily and the Galleys of Naples; forces that had an important role in the battle of Lepanto or the expedition to San Salvador in

"Galicia"

The L51 is a modern amphibiaious transport vessel designed by the National Company Bazán to fulfill the needs of the Spanish navy. This entered into service in 1998 since when it has been used both in humanitarian actions and in the deployment of troops in peace missions.

Brazil. In 1704, they were organized into regiments, receiving the denomination of Bajeles, Armada, Naples Sea and Sicilian Sea, and in 1717 artillery elements were formed to support them. The troops of the IM fought to re-conquer Buenos Aires in Argentina in 1806, battled against Napoleon, intervened in the first Carlist war and took part in the Cuban Campaign of 1875 and 1898.

In the 20th century various changes took place, one of the most important being the

Equipment

The equipment of the Spanish marine infantry is noted for its excellent quality and for including all the necessary elements to carry out tasks. In the photograph, a soldier covers his face and arms with camouflage paint.

ARMORED RECONNAISSANCE VEHICLE SCORPION

In 1985, as result of the good performance during the Falklands war, Spain decided to incorporate 17 of the British lightweight SCORPION armored vehicle. This vehicle that stands out for its reduced weight, great agility in the most varied of terrains and the ability to carry three men together with a 76 mm gun that allows it to confront other armored vehicles.
This vehicle, of which more than 2000 have been produced and distributed to over 20 countries, stands out for its tracked-wheel undercarriage sustained by 5 driving wheels on either side, for its Perkins engine at
the front to make it more resistant to direct impact; for having armor capable of resisting guided missiles of 7.62 mm and 14.5 mm with its frontal arch and for weighing a little more than 8 tons. Also significant is its advanced targeting and resources that allow it to circulate and fight even at night, for this reason it is ideal for armored reconnaissance actions in spearheading Marine Infantry troops and because they can easily be transported from amphibian vessels to the beaches where they move with exceptional freedom.

creation, at the end of the Civil War, of the Northern Corps in Ferrol, the Southern Corps at San Fernando, the Eastern Coast Corps at Cartagena, those of the Balearic Islands in Mallorca and of the Canaries at Las Palmas de Gran Canaria. In 1957, the special support groups and application school was formed. In 1967, the TEAR was formed and in 1996 the E-01 plan approved the formation of the BRIMAR. This force will be completely operative in the first years of the 21st century, nevertheless, since 1996 they have collaborated in peace-keeping activities in Bosnia.

Effective organization

The General Command of the TEAR, (GETEAR) that reports to the General Commander of the IM (COMGEIM) is in charge of various organizations amongst which is BRINMAR that is responsible for providing the troops that will make up landing forces. It is made up of a General Staff (EM), the General Headquarters (UCG), two battalions of disembarkment, the Special Operations Unit (UOE), the Artillery Disembarkment Unit (GAD) the Mechanical Amphibious Unit (GMA) and the Combat Support Group (GASC).

The EM includes sections of personnel (1st section), intelligence, (2nd section), operations, (3rd section), logistics (4th section) and communications (5th sec-

tion). As for the UCG, which provides the capacity for command, control and intelligence to the Brigade (C21), this is composed of the following companies: the General Headquarters which includes security platoons of the Military Police, an Intelligence company that consists of elements to obtain data such as personnel locating radars or thermic cameras and the communications company that is noted for its sections of Radio, Telephones, Electronic War and the Communications Center (CECOM) in which parabolic antennae for satellite connections are used. Amphibious assault is the task commended to both the first landing Battalion (BDI) and the second (BDII). They include some 700 people in each and are commanded by a Lieutenant Colonel, and structured as follows: a Company PLM and of Services in which the Reconnaissance Sections (SERECO) and of Communications stand out using sophisticated equipment of PR4G type, a Company of Armaments with medium mortars of 81 mm, anti-tank tank missile launchers of short range and heavy machine guns and three Infantry companies. Each one includes 169 personnel that make up three rifle sections and one of armaments, and for immediate support rely on light and medium machine guns, 60 mm mortars and disposable rocket launchers. To complement these two battalions the creation of a BDE-III is currently being undertaken. This will differ from the other two in that it will be mecha-

Training

At the San Fernando camp there is an area incorporating a training track. There the men improve their physical condition and practice movements that are inherent to their deployment as a Marine Infantry Force.

Support

In those tactical situations where fast and decisive fire support is required, this light ECIA mortars M86 of 60 mm are very useful. These can be carried in a harness located on the shoulders of the soldiers responsible for firing them.

nized and will have larger and more powerful firing elements and improved protection; furthermore it will be distributed between the two companies of Mechanized Infantry and the Combat Tank Company.

Insofar as the EOU is concerned, this includes three specialized sections; the GAD in charge of providing support fire and carrying out anti-aircraft defense, for which it has towed items, self-propelled howitzers and anti-aircraft missiles, elements that are complemented with equipment for Acquiring and Location of Support Fire (ACAF) and the centers for Directing Fire (FDC). As for the GMA this groups the companies of command

and PLM, Anti-tank weapons, Amphibious Assault Tractors, Medium Tanks and Armored Reconnaissance Vehicles.

Finally, the GASC provides the necessary logistic support that the Brigade

needs, for which it divides its resources between the companies of Command and PLM, Supply, Maintenance, Organization and Movement on Beaches or OMP, Auto Transport, Medical and Sappers, in total more than 500 men.

The future organization contemplates the creation of a Special Arms Group (GAE) into which Sappers, amphibian assault vehicles and long range anti-tanks missiles will be integrated, along with the Aerial Group of the IM (GRAIM) which will have bi-dimensional detection radars and will be assigned a Unit of Transport Helicopters. This will coordinate the use of the Augusta Bell AB-2212 that at present is assigned to the 3rd Squadron.

Night
The Brigade of the Marine Infantry has AN/PVS-7D night vision goggles of United States origin. They include III Generation captation and an infra-red illuminator that allows for vision at locations without residual light.

Power
The Tank Company includes seventeen United States medium tanks M60A3 TTS. Capable of transporting a crew of four people, it has a 105 mm gun, and its almost 800 horsepower diesel engine permits it to move freely at the beach-head.

Supranational organizations

The training of the new BRIMAR has been carried out coinciding with that of a new common policy for the joint defense of Europe. In this context, Spain has signed a bilateral agreement with Italy thus creating the SIAF (Spanish-Italian Amphibious Force), an agreement that was formalized in a ceremony at the port of Bar-

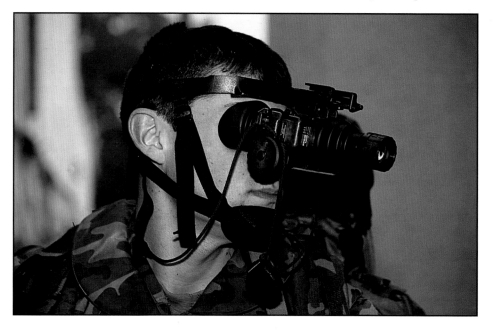

ANTI-TANK MISSILE SYSTEM TOW 2

At the beginning of the 1980's the Spanish Marine Infantry received a dozen launchers of the United States anti-tank missile TOW, weapons which they installed on Land Rover vehicles. In time, these were substituted by the more powerful and capable HUMMER, which are configured as follows: Two system operators that act under the protection of the armor, a carriage for the transport of half a dozen missiles in their containers and mounts providing the launcher and associated equipment with freedom of movement.

For firing, it is only necessary to place the launcher at the muzzle and proceed to recharge a container tube, an action normally carried out behind the shelter of the
armor at the rear. The system is wire-guided and has a target range of 3,750 m. Its guidance system has a thermal scope that enables it to be used at night and in adverse climatic conditions.

In order to improve these characteristics, since 1999 a change has been made to the TOW-2 model, which incorporates a more modern guidance system. Some of its components have also been improved, for example the missile which now includes a larger and more powerful war-head of larger diameter and strength with which it can face up to protected elements better. In the next few years it is hoped to increase the actual number of existing launchers with another dozen making a total of 24.

celona in 1998. It has also been decided that Spain will participate in the CAFMED (Combined Amphibious Forces of the Mediterranean) proposed by NATO in order to support the CJTF (Combined Joint Task Forces) and the EUROMANFOR, the European Naval Forces.

Continous training

The BRIMAR is made up of 4,151 men and women trained to carry out specific tasks that require a high level of preparation and personal involvement, for this reason in their training there is included both an amphibious phase and a terrestrial phase.

In the first, which usually takes place at the San Fernando camp or at nearby locations such as La Clica or at the Firing and Maneuvers Range at Retín, they endeavor

to reach three levels: individual preparation, group and integrated. In the first the soldiers seek aptitudes and knowledge so that can carry out tasks inherently related to a specific post within an organic structure.

In their group training they seek the integration of individual actions into the different organizations: the squadron, platoon, the section or the company. They work at Battalion or Group level, a phase in which they also work with terrestrial and aerial resources.

The integrated level aims for the units of combat, of combat support and service support to work together in a joint and coordinated manner; for this, different exercises are programmed which range from the level of the reinforced Battalion for landing to that of Brigade. This way, it is easier to implement the efficiency of the organs of Command and of systems for Command and Control in simulation of actions that would take place in the battle-field.

With respect to purely amphibious training, the idea is that the infantry work with the vessels that will transport and deploy them in actions and missions that will be assigned to them. In the initial pha-se, and so that they become familiarized with procedures and characteristics, they practice embarking and disembarking in port which permits them to carry out tasks such as the embarking of vehicles, the sto-wage of equipment or the placing of the troops in the holds. The advanced phase includes navigation and disembarking, both national and multi-national of which we can outline titles such as "Adelfibex, Anfibex, Dynamic Mix, Phiblex, Destined Glory or Tapón".

The previous phases include inter-

Defense
The Spanish Marine Infantry deploys twelve launchers of the French anti-aircraft missile system Mistral, armaments that are mobilized by HUMMER vehicles and that also trans-port containers with additional infra-red missiles.

Assault
The capacity of the Navy includes ships and aircraft with which they can sup-port the assaults of the marine infantry on coasts or hostile locations. It is nor-mal for infiltration by sea to be accom-panied by helicopters transport.

mixed cycles in order that the newer per-sonnel advance in training and overlap with those who have more experience, concentrating the personnel in those com-panies according to a higher or lower level of training. In this way, it is possible to maintain a high percentage of the Brigade at an optimum level for action, and another part is maintained in reserve for when they may be needed.

Finally it is to be noted that the member officers of the IM extend the training they receive at the Marine Military School with further tuition such as the Amphibian Ope-rations course that they undertake at the Marine Infantry School at San Fernando.

The non-commissioned officers derive from the core of the Professional Military Troops (MTP's); those who have entered at a lower level and want to have access to a higher post can do so by means of an exa-mination. They undertake their specific instruction at the Non Commissioned Offi-cer's School and at the EIM, where they can follow complementary courses in spe-cialties such as: Artillery, Automobiles, Communications, Mechanized Amphibian Means or Engineers.

Modern and varied resources
The equipment of the Spanish marine soldiers is noted out for its quality and variety. With regard to the uniform, alt-hough during 1999 they have started to

receive new mimetic clothing in tones that are very similar to those of the US, the following is the most important: belting that is similar to that of ALICE (All purpose Lightweight Carry Equipment), an anti-flack jacket and other clothing that is complemented with the *teresiana*, the beret made out of the same material as the uniform, the Marte helmet, leather gloves, the large capacity Altus rucksacks, the individual protection equipment EPI, battle jackets made of Gore-Tex or of polar lining.

The armament consists of: assault rifle CETME L that will be replaced by the Heckler und Köch G36 E from the year 2000; Llama M82 and Star 30 M pistols; precision rifles C75 and Accuracy AW,

Assault
From the amphibious ships, such as the L-42 Pizarro, launches may be released with troops for Landing or to facilitate the deployment of amphibious assault tractors. The stern has a ramp that permits the direct placing of vehicles onto the beach or via floating pontoons.

large caliber Barrett M-95, PO and Calderón grenades, Instalaza rifle grenades T5; disposable C-90C/CR rocket launchers;

AMELI light machine guns; medium MG42 and FN MAG; and M-2 HB and M85, light ECIA mortars M86 60 mm; and 81 mm medium mortars. On some of the above mentioned can be fitted diurnal firing scopes such as the L9 SUSAT (Sight Unit, Small Arms Trilux), Carl Zeiss Diavari, Habbit Barret 10 x 42 and Smith & Bender 3-12 x 50; for night use are the Simrad Kn-202F Mk 3, AN/PVS-4 and AN/TVS-5 that are complemented by AN/PVS-7D goggles.

In order to deploy firearms in the battle field they use towed howitzers Oto-Melara M56 of 105/14; self-propelled howitzers M109A2 of 155/32 drawn by caterpillar vehicles, ammunition M992 FAASV; short range missile launchers M-47 DRAGON and long range TOW-2; carriages for the anti-aircraft missile MISTRAL; amphibian tractors AAV-7 A1; armored reconnaissance vehicles SCORPION FV 101; and medium combat tanks M60A3 TTS.

Other elements that support the capacity for deployment and combat consist

of Global positioning systems (GPS), rapid landing Duarry Supercat with two 90 horsepower engines; 4th generation communication equipment Thompson-CSF PR4G, portable and mobile computers that allow connections via the HIS-PASAT and INMARSAT satellites; remote RACAL Classic 2000 sensors; Infametrics IRTV 445L thermal cameras; ARI-NE localization radars; all terrain vehicles AM General HUMMER in various versions that include ambulances, or armored tactical Pegaso and Iveco lorries that weight 3 and 6 tons. Tractor-lorries Kynos Aljaba that transport CT-50 L vessels; containers and cabins for specific equipment; mobile showers and kitchens; mechanical mules TITAN MV-3 and MM-1 A and heavy machinery such as

Resistance

The troops of the Marine Infantry are made up of men who are noted for their physical agility and for their resistance. These are qualities that, when participating in amphibious assaults, permit them to demonstrate their capacity for combat in difficult and adverse situations.

Mobility

Two hundred HUMMER vehicles guarantee the mobility of the troops or the associated system of armament (in this case, a TOW missile launcher) in the most difficult of terrain. These vehicles are characterized by their great power, agility and high potential for use.

forklifts, power shovels, bulldozers and retro-excavators.

In order to transport these in exercises, maneuvers or in actual actions, Delta group vessels are available, including: LPD's (Landing Platform Dock) L-51 Galicia and L-52 Castilla which enter into service during the year 2000, and LST (Landing Ship Tank) Hernán Cortés and Pizarro. In the near future, these vessels will be complemented with a LPH (Landing Platform Helicopter) currently known as: L-53. From these vessels, launches type LCVP, LCU, LCM-6 and LCM-8, are released and from the deck, Helicopters type AB-212 and SH-3H are operated, permitting them to move groups of infantry swiftly to the beachhead.

The Spanish Marine Infantry Brigade (BRIMAR), is a special Naval Operations element known as UOE made up of somewhat more than 100 men trained in a wide variety of techniques: manual parachuting, diving, explosives, target reconnaissance or navigation with the aid of mini-submarines for infiltration .

Fifty years of history

Since its creation in 1952 the UOE has substantially changed its professional capacity and the resources used in comparison with those of 1952. Its history coincides with the creation of an Amphibious Scaling Company that was formed in the Northern Regiment (TERNOR) at Ferrol in order to have the capability of attacking any hostile coast, no matter how difficult.

Change of headquarters to Cádiz

This company formed by command staff and three operative units, was moved from Ferrol to Chiclana in 1957 and integrated into the Special Marine Infantry

Discretion
The Spanish naval commandos use for their night time missions, 2nd or 3rd generation binoculars and Sterling rifles that carry an integrated silencer. These allow them to move and to combat without giving away their whereabouts.

Group, forerunner of the actual TEAR. At the beginning of the 60's they moved to a base in San Fernando and in 1966 it was decided to change the name to Special Operations Company led by Captain Julio Yánez Golf, thereby commencing a change in working mentality, operative techniques and assigned missions.

In 1969, its denomination changed to Special Unit Operations and its organization was modified to include sections of Amphibian Sappers, Reconnaissance and Assault and Combat Divers. That same year saw its deployment in the contingents that covered the evacuations of Equatorial Guinea and Sidi Ifni (Morocco).

Three years later a Ministerial Order was approved which declared the green beret to be obligatory for its members and in 1974 it was reorganized under the leadership of Commander Gorordo. These changes motivated changes in the command of its three sections to pass from

that of Lieutenant to Captain and its name was changed to Special Unit Amphibious Incursions (UNESIAN). In 1974, they intervened in another operation in the Sahara in order to study beaches for a possible landing.

In 1983 the name was changed once again to Special Amphibious Command (COMANFES). The rank of its commander was elevated to that of Lieutenant Colonel and its organization was based upon three special operations units, recovering its designation of UOE in 1988. In 1996, as had occurred in the Guinean or Somalian crisis, an operative team was deployed to Bosnia-Herzegovina, a mission that continued until the end of 1999.

Complete profesionalization

Since 1993 its operative units have been made up of professionals that can maintain and increase their capacity for as long as they are deployed. The slogan "In the UOE enter only those who can and not those who want to" is indicative of the difficulty of obtaining a post in this operative unit.

The soldiers seeking entry have to pass the Special Operations Aptitude Test for Professional Militaries (MEPT). It lasts for three months and includes an initial phase of physical and psycho-technical tests, another of basic instruction that increases their physical and psychological resistance, and an advanced instruction

phase in which they learn climbing techniques, naval skills or reconnaissance patrol skills.

At the end, normally less than 10 % of the 40 who enter obtain the qualification that will permit them to proceed to the automatic parachuting course and obtain the long awaited green beret which identifies them.

The commanding officers must pass the higher level aptitude test for the staff of Special Operations Units, which is carried out in the Military Mountain and Special Operations School (EMMOE) in Jaca for ten months from September to June each year. This very tough and tech-

SIG-SAUER PISTOL P230

The Swiss Industrial Company SIG and the German J. P. Sauer and Sohn have collaborated for many years in the manufacture of a highly reputed collection of short and medium firearms. Amongst the first we find the semi automatic pistol P230 which can be used in double and simple action and which is fed with a magazine with capacity for 7 cartridges caliber 9x17 mm. Its basic weight is about 460 grams to which 200 more have to be added when considering the elongated barrel for the model as used by the UOE. This barrel considerably reduces the noise associated with

the detonation particularly if subsonic ammunition is used and this prevents a shot from giving away the presence of an attacking force. It also includes an anchorage cord fixed to the lower part in order to prevent falls during the rapid movements of the amphibious Spanish green berets. At the top of the barrel there are aiming elements with a radius between sights of 120 mm. In order to fire in simple action a force of 17 Newtons is required that rises to 45 in double action and the gun includes 6 chambers with a spacing of every 25 cms.

Movements

For their deployment in coastal areas, several types of boats are used, amongst these stand out the pneumatic launches Zodiac F470 that are propelled by 35-40 horse power out-board engines placed at the stern.

nical apprenticeship will allow them to later form part of the units and carry out training that will improve their personal qualification and of those under their command, such exercises, both national and multinational, demand the carrying out of the most diverse of activities.

Their participation in other special courses such as combat diving, High Altitude High Opening, (HAHO) or High Altitude Low Opening (HALO) parachuting, those of targeting of objectives or Forward Air Controller (FAC) or of deactivation of explosives under water, is notable.

Equipment adapted to their activity

In order to carry out all these activities

and to guarantee the capacity for intervention in any circumstance, the UOE has been given a collection of arms, equip-

ment and very advanced systems that permit those integrated into the unit to yield their maximum level of productivity.

Arms and special systems

The collection of arms deployed by these naval commandos is very large and includes pistols Llam M-82 and SIG Sauer P-230; sub-rifles Sterling MK 5 with silencer to which can be added the Hecker und Kock MP5; assault rifles CETME LV with SUSAT scope and the M-16, light machine guns AMELI 5.56 and the medium MG-42 and M-60 both of 7.62; precision rifles Mauser 66 and Accuracy AW, the anti-material Barret

Assault

The heavy helicopters SH-3H Sea King of the Aircraft Fleet of the Air Arm of the Navy are used to transport the Spanish naval commandos to the place where the attacks will commence. Depending on where they land and the conditions, they may use the 'fast rope' technique to lower them to the ground.

rifle M-95 of 12.70 and the Remington Wingmaster M870 shotgun caliber 12. In some, lasers have been added for instinctive aiming and as more forceful elements Calderón Grenades and Instalaza C-90C/CR rocket launchers are used.

Of personal equipment mention may be made of the tactical jackets to transport the basic elements for action; Marte bullet proof helmets and bullet and flack proof jackets; wetsuits and all the necessary elements for diving, automatic and manual parachutes with all complements and oxygen for high altitude parachuting. Night vision glasses AN/PVS-7B, Maguellán and Trimble Scout, satellite receivers and laser beam EISA LP7. To support general activities use is made of dismountable Kayacks, (IBS) Inflatable Boat System boats and Zodiac F470 Commando. Four wheeled Hummer and a great variety of communication equipment of which the French PR4G and the American digital Harris Corporation AN/PRC-139 stand out.

Infiltration
The Navy's submarines can carry small command groups to the point of infiltration, where with the aid of pneumatic boats, they will initiate their move to the coast. Once there, they will start to carry out their mission and later extricate themselves.

Undertaking the most varied of missions.

The operatives of the three operational units, to which an administrative staff dedicated to services must be added, are in charge of the carrying out of direct action missions and of special reconnaissance. The first concerns offensive attacks on valuable tactical, operational and strategic objectives, the second seeks information.

They are organized into special or amphibian reconnaissance patrols (respectively PRE or ART), carry out the Non-Combatant Evacuation Operation

Manual operation
All the members of the UOE are prepared for the automatic parachute jump, and a high percentage are prepared for the manual opening parachute jump. To practice this technique of infiltration, they usually transfer to the base of Alcantarilla where they work with Aviocars type C-212.

(NEO), recovery of personnel in enemy territory both in the Tactical Recovery of Aircraft and/or Personal (TRAP) and Combat, Search and Rescue (CSAR) and undertake exercises in assault and boarding vessels. (BOARDEX, Boarding Exercise). For these exercises they use patrol boats or submarines, they infiltrate from aircraft or helicopters, or navigate with SDV mini-submarines (Swimmers Delivery Vehicle).

ROYAL MARINES, BRITISH AMPHIBIOUS TROOPS

The United Kingdom has a very professional army equipped with highly sophisticated materials and its historical tradition with regard to the deployment and potential to undertake the most varied type of combat or mission is deeply rooted.

Within these forces is found the disembarking force known as Royal Marines (RM) and integrated into the Royal Navy, currently with some 7000 troops reporting to the General Headquarters situated in the CTCRM in the Isle of Whale, Portsmouth. This force accounts for some 17 % of the manpower of the Royal Navy.

Advanced training

The men and women who make up this highly qualified Infantry Unit, with a large capacity for amphibious deployment, all pass through the Commando Training Center RM (CTCRM) located at Lympstone, Devon.

Transport

The British Royal Navy has enough resources for the deployment of its Commando troops; amongst the vessels in service is found the L11 Fearless which became famous for its participation in the Falklands war in 1982.

Preparation of its members

These installations have their origin in a training camp for reservists established in 1939 and received its actual name in 1970. Its mission is to train officers, non-commissioned officers and soldiers in every aspect including basic and advanced areas; there are also courses for promotion of non-commissioned officers and specific courses of preparation for the multiple requirements of this Corps.

Characteristics

The Royal Marines Commando are troops made up of military professionals, well trained and perfectly equipped. They have many years experience in peace-keeping missions, combat deployment and security.

Devon is the site of the Officer's Training Wing, the Infantry Support Wing, the Non-Commissioned Officer's Training Wing and the Personnel Commando Training Wing for amphibious personnel. The preparation of the Young Officers (YO's) who may enlist for either a short or long period, includes 14 months of studies at the CTCRM that serves to develop leadership, character and the necessary qualities to lead an operational unit of RM that consist of 28 non commissioned officers. For their part university cadets have to pass an initial 3 week training course at the CTCRM before applying to University, training which is complemented with two similar periods each year until they graduate and can start the rest of their training with the rest of the YO's.

The Infantry Support Wing consists of an Armed Platoon (PW), an Assault Engineer Platoon (AE), a Heavy Arms Section

(HW) and the Field Support platoons, PT and Instruction; it also includes the Association of Sporting Parachutist of the Royal Navy and Marines. The above mentioned have the task of training the arms and troop platoons; the preparation of assault engineers, select marksmen, handlers of 81 mm medium mortars and operators of the MILAN anti-tank missile, or training in areas of heavy armament, Nuclear, Bacteriological and Chemical war (NBQ) or rock climbing.

In the Non-Commissioned Officer's Training Wing diverse courses are provided for the promotion of members of the active army, the Reserve and the Band. The training consists of 4 different levels: the Junior Command Course (JCC) to promote Corporals, the Senior Command Course (SCC) for Sergeants, the Advanced Command Course (ACC) that promotes selected Sergeants to Warrant Officer WO2, and the RSM that allows the above mentioned to promote to the rank of Sergeant Major of the regiments.

The responsibility for training the recruits that wish to become part of the RM is that of the Commando Training Wing, requiring 30 weeks to prepare this contingent who receive the basic training for infantry of the North Atlantic Treaty Organization (NATO).

In order to carry out this process, which usually includes groups of 50 per-

MEDIUM MACHINE GUN L7

In those areas where powerful and sustained firing is required, usually undertaken by the support platoons, the robust L7A2 machine guns are used. These are manufactured by the Royal Small Arms in its factory at Enfield Lock. This weapon is the English version of the Belgian model MAG on which it is based, however the spare parts are not interchangeable. Its design makes it possible to fire belted ammunition caliber 7.62x51 mm at a rate of 750–1000 rounds per minute and its 679 mm rifled barrel provides a firing velocity of 838 mts per second at exit. This armament has a weight of 10.9 kgs, including a grip on the top to facilitate transport and incorporates a front and rear regulable elevating sight that facilitates aiming particularly if fired from a tripod that ensures stability.
The L7A2 has given rise to many variations adapted to its use as an infantry armament or for secondary use in tanks or vehicles. Noteable variants include the L19A1 incorporating a more robust barrel.

sons, the wing is subdivided into three companies; those of Porstmouth, Chatham and Plymouth, the first two being in charge of training and the last the administration of the training process.

Three centuries of activity

The Royal Marine's history is laden with victories and glorious acts. It was constituted during the reign of Charles II on 28th October 1664 when a regiment for the admiralty was formed. One of its first victories was the capture of Gibraltar in 1704 and its defense during the 9 months that the besieging of the rock lasted, forming a coalition with Dutch troops that were fighting the Spanish War of Succession at the time.

In the 18th and 19th centuries the Corps took part in the majority of wars that were fought that enabled the creation of the British Empire and this led them to form part of the elements that bombarded Algeria in 1816. They participated in the Ashanti wars, saw themselves involved in the destruction of the Turkish fleet in Navarino in 1827 and took part in the Crimean war and the besieging of Sebastopol in 1854.

Hovercraft
In order to facilitate rapid transport from the amphibian vessels to the coast, various resources are used, one of these is the Griffon 2000 TDX, a hovercraft capable of transporting 16 soldiers or two tons of equipment at at speeds of up to 30 knots.

In the 20th century they played a significant role in the First World War (1914-1918) and the military units of the RM made up the groups responsible for the manipulation of weapons and guns in vessels larger than that of destroyer, participating with more than 5,700 in the Battle of Jutland. They also participated in the battles of Gallipoli, Zeebruge and in the trenches of the Western Front.

During the first three years of the Second World War (1939-45), they formed part of the crews of ships and from 1942 the first Commandos were formed, a designation that bears no relation to the special troops being deployed in Sicily, The Dalmatian Coast, Salerno, Anzio, Termoly, Burma or India. Five RM Commando units were disembarked on D day, reaching a total of 80,000 men by the end of the conflict.

Contact
In order to maintain contact between the disembarked elements, the deployed patrols, the transport vessels and aerial support, it is necessary to deploy an important network of communications equipment that allow transmission both ground-to-ground and ground-to-air.

Since then, the presence of the 3rd Commando Brigade during the crisis in Palestine, the Malayan campaign or the problems and fighting in Brunei, Korea, Cyprus, Tanganyika or Borneo are of particular note. From 1969 they have been deployed in Northern Ireland to halt the radical IRA terrorist group. In 1981 the withdrawal of the two LPD vessels from the RN was approved, as also to reduce the number of Marines, but their role in the events that took place in 1982 when the Argentines invaded the Falkland Islands, was decisive in recovering British Sovereignty in those southern terrritories.

More recent are the deployments in Saudi Arabia on the occasion of the Gulf war; in Kurdish Iraq, during the humanitarian operation Haven; in Bosnia-Herzegovina to carry out missions of pacification; or in Brazzaville in 1997, for the possible

Helicopters
The Westland Sea King are medium transport helicopters, that can carry up to 24 completely equipped marines. They have been improved to stay in service until 2010 with self-defense electronic equipment. They were used by the ISFOR during the Yugoslav crisis.

Heavyweight
The soldiers' equipment is heavy and voluminous, therefore they use large rucksacks that can carry food, clothing, ammunition, complementary equipment, etc. up to 40 Kgs in weight.

evacuation of British and other Commonwealth citizens.

3rd Commando Brigade
This is an amphibious force of light infantry, with the entity of a Brigade. and made up of 4,132 persons. It is commanded by a Brigadier and stands out for its capacity to carry out military actions in mountains or in conditions of extreme cold It usually operates independently or in joint organizations such as the Joint Rapid Deployment Force (JRDF) or the Anglo-Dutch amphibious force that is configured jointly with the Royal Netherlands Marine Corps (RNIMC), for exercises and to be activated in the event of war.

Structure and organization
This brigade consists of: a General Headquarters, an element of Headquarters and Communications with communication sections, reconnaissance patrols, electronic war, anti-aircraft defense, police and tacti-

cal control; three Marine Battalions known as Commando and identified by the numbers 40, 42 and 45, The artillery formed by the 29 Commando Regiment Royal Artillery, the defense anti-aircraft battery of the 20 Commando Battery Royal Artillery; the 59 Engineering Squadron backed by the 139 reserve; the logistic regiment grouped into a Commando; the 539 Assault squadron and the 845, 846 and 847 Naval Air Squadrons; the three Comman-

do type infantry units correspond to light battalions that make up the maneuver elements of the Brigade and give them their capacity for action, with some 600 men in each; the artillery units are in charge of fire support and anti-aircraft defense for which they have 24 towed howitzers L115 Light Gun of 105/37 mm

Beach
After the amphibian elements reach the beach and consolidate the positions assigned in the assault, the preparation of the support elements begins. They are deployed in various vehicles and systems that include the tracked dual cabin Bv-206.

and 10 low level Rapier anti-aircraft defense systems, these elements being complemented by a battery of medium range 81 mm mortars; the logistic elements include four squadrons assigned to transport, medical assistance, repair and diverse support. For their part the aerial units consist of : a light helicopter squadron with four Lynx anti-tank functions, eight reconnaissance Gazelle and two of medium transport with 16 Westland Sea King HC4 Commando. Aircraft that will be complemented or substituted by those of attack WAH-64D Apache in the near future, adapted to the marine environment and also those of transport EH-101 Merlin that it is hoped will be incorporated during 2006.

Assault
The light Westland Lynx Mk 7 Helicopters are used to move certain groups of troops or to give mobility to particular arms systems. It is possible to deploy the soldiers to the ground by rappel or fast rope techniques.

In the Brigade, are also found the special operations element defined as Comancchio Group. Based in the Scottish town of Arbroath, its principal task is to provide marines for the security of nuclear submarines based at the Clyde. They carry out patrols as well as maintaining a rapid reaction team, who usually train in patrol activities in Northern Ireland. This unit regularly carries out exercises in Cyprus and United States with elements of the US Marine Corps. In support of the brigade is the Special Boat Service (SBS), a force trained to carry out special operations that initiate at sea and directed towards the coast.

The General Headquarters and the elements of communication occupy installations at Stonehouse, Plymouth, the 40th Command is based at Norton Manor Camp

Defense

To guarantee self-defense of vital points from possible attacks of the enemy planes, individual and triple launchers of the Javelin anti-aircraft short range missile systems are normally used. These arms are denominated "shoot and forget" because they automatically target the objective.

in Taunton, the 42nd Command at Bickley, Plymouth, the 45th Commando is at Arbroath and the logistic regiment is based at Chivenor.

Yeovilton is the location of the 847 Naval Air Squadron, the 539 Assault Squadron is based at Turnchapel in Plymouth, The Comacchio Group is based in Arbroath, in Poole is found the SBS and the training wing for amphibian disembarking. The Training Unit RM (ATTURM) the training and testing amphibious unit is located at Instow. Likewise threre are also elements of the RM based in Germany, Australia, Barbados, Belgium, Bosnia, Brunei, Canada, Cyprus, Diego García, United States, Gibraltar, Holland, Kuwait, Latvia, Norway, Oman and Thailand.

As a complement and support to the troops in active service, the Royal Marines Reserve (RMR) exists formed by men and women that voluntarily serve and dedicate part of their time to training and preparing themselves for combat. It's anticipated size is of 1,580 people, but at present amounts to only 1.200. When seeking to enter into the RMR an undertaking for four years is required, period which may be increased. They are based in locations such as: Porstmouth, Bermondsey, Newcastle, Dundee,

Elite

Within the Royal Marines Commando are integrated specialist units that carry out in depth reconnaissance tasks, assault, destruction, parachuting, diving and combat in the most varied scenarios. They are the special forces, and amongst their armaments is found the M-16 equipped with 40 mm grenade launchers M-203 of 40 mm.

DUAL-CABIN TRACKED VEHICLE BV-210

In the last few years, the Royal Marines have used several hundred Swedish vehicles type Bv-206. These dual-cabin tracked vehicles stand out for their adaptation to missions such as logistical elements or as mobile communication centers. In 1999 the acquisition of 164 ATV's (All Terrain Vehicles) was approved, and it was decided that the model that corresponded to the requirements of the RM was the Bv-210 that, as before, is manufactured by Hägglunds Vehicle.

This is an articulated double cabin that inherits the design of the Bv-206S. Manufactured with armored steel, it has been given more angular and lower forms that make its localization more difficult and provide it with a higher survival level from the impact of lightweight arms and the flack derived from explosions of howitzers or grenades. They weigh about 7 tons and are partially amphibious so that they may reach the shore by their own means after disembarking from vessels. They are capable of providing mobility to a dozen men with equipment and its maximum load capacity is almost 2 tons.

A mount is situated on the upper part for the location of diverse types of weapons, and its thick armored glass permits unrestricted observation with the knowledge that they will stand impacts of up to 7.62 mm caliber.

Bristol, Lympstone, Devonport, Birmingham, Glasgow, Edinburgh and Birkenhead.

Equiment and mobility

The equipment is modern and diverse, and ranges from the most significant of assault rifles SA-80 and M-16 caliber 5.56 (.223 Remington), to medium machine guns. L7 of 7.62 x 51 mm (.308 Winchester), precision accuracy rifles AW 7.62 Barrett M82A1 caliber 12.70 x 99 mm (.50 Browning), heavy machine guns M-2 HB 12,70, monotube grenade launchers M203 of 40 mm, monotube and tritube missile launchers of the Javelin anti-aircraft system, wire guided medium range anti-tank systems MILAN, two hundred tracked vehicles BV 206 that will be replaced in the coming months by the armored version BVS-10 of this Swedish dual cabin machine, and more than a thousand wheeled vehicles. In coming months they also hope to receive 40 mm automatic grenade launchers that will be employed from both fixed and mobile mounts.

Amongst recently acquired elements, are found 40 Divex respirators of a variant type for the use of combat divers and deactivators of explosives that have maximum depths of use of 40 m and 100 m respectively. They stand out for their reduced volume and float more easily and permit an easier control of floatability with an autonomy lasting for four hours with a breathing rate of 35 liters per minute. These artifacts are particularly useful in operating in mini-submarines assigned to the marines of the SBS who possess three mini-submarines type SDV Mk 8 model 1 that have a 50 % higher range than the 0 model that was used a few years ago.

To ensure the free movement of the marine force, reliance is made on an amphibious force made up of the LPD (Landing Platform Dock) L 10 Fearless, which can transport nearly 17.000 tons. Five vessels type Sir Bedivere and Sir Galahad assigned to logistic transport and the modern Landing Platform Helicopter (LPH L12) Ocean that displaces 21,758 tons. This stands out for its elongated deck allowing 7 helicopters to take off at the same time in order to deploy their load a coastal area. From 2002 the L 14 Albion and L15 Bulwark will come into action, both LPD's of great capacity and modern design.

From the above, launches type Landing Craft Utility (LCU) Mk9, and the LandingCraft Vehicles and Personal (LCVP) Mk4 and Mk5, and the Hovercrafts Griffon 2000 TDX are used. To these will be added shortly 10 launches LCU Mk 10 ordered in 1998 from BAE-SEMA and they also hope to incorporate large capacity vessels type LCVP (Lan-

Support
The maintenance of a force strong enough to dislodge the enemy from the beachhead until he retreats, demands the support of many logistical elements, in particular in the support to troops and provision of munitions armament systems.

ding Craft Air Cushion). These will complement the Westland Sea King and Lynx in the rapid transport of marines to the coast.

Logistics
The Royal Navy has a considerable force of amphibian vessels dedicated to the transport of troops or logistical back-up. A task carried out by the L3036 Sir Percivale and another four vessels of similar characteristics, all named after the knights of the Round Table.

ROYAL NETHERLANDS MARINES

Holland, being a small country as far as extension goes, is one of the most densely populated countries in Europe. Its geo-strategic position, with a low and sandy coast line, its strong industrial economy and the desire to maintain the highest level of self-defense has led to the creation of efficient and well equipped armed forces.

Of the three main components of the armed forces the Navy or the Royal Netherlands Navy stands out, with a Rear-Admiral as commander.

It counts on an excellent submarine and surface fleet backed by logistic and auxiliary vessels and to which the modern Rotterdam were added in 1998 in order to facilitate the movements of its own corps of marines.

Prepared and efficient amphibious force

The history of this unit dates back to 1665 with the creation of the Marines Corps by Michiel de Ryter and Johan de

Targeting
The use of optical scopes on the DIE-MACO C7 assault rifles favors the soldiers capacity to shoot effectively to targets of short and medium range. A distance at which the .223 mm Remington ammunition has a proven capability.

Wit who thought of the necessity to have military force that could protect the interests of Holland throughout the world, as its motto "Quo Pater Orbis" makes clear.

Prepared for combat
Amongst the approximately 16,000 members of the Marine, 3,000 can be identified as making up the actual Royal Marine Corps. Although specialized in amphibian operations, they can carry out many more tasks under the most varied of conditions and in the most remote of areas. Thus, these marines are prepared to operate with assault vessels, transported and disembarked by helicopter, or to be laun-

ched by parachute at the point where the force is to be deployed. All of these actions require a careful selection of members who undergo a high level of physical and military training.

They also carry out other activities ranging from participation in the opening ceremony of parliament, that takes place each year at the beginning of September, to the manipulation of the light boats of many of the military surface vessels. These activities require a constant training of the troops, involving an initial phase that lasts for 21 weeks at the Van Ghent camp in Rotterdam and completed by an amphibious phase at the Joost Dourlein camp. They then specialize as ski instructors, parachutists select marksmen, fitters, signallers, etc. The officers who have contracts for indefinite periods of service undertake a course at the Royal Naval College of Den Helder.

Once integrated into the operative units they carry out single and combined

Snow
The Dutch marines usually carry out exercises in the proximity of Norway where the climatic conditions are very adverse. This training allows them to improve the physical capacity of their men and to put to the test the resistance of the assigned resources.

Support
The FN MAG machine guns of the Royal Marines are noteable for firing belted ammunition of caliber 7.62 x 51 mm. It includes a transportation grip at the top and counts on a bipod that stabilizes firing and thus obtaining a better grouping of shots.

exercises that will take them to diverse scenarios.

Among locations these is Northern Norway, an area of extreme climatic conditions and rough seas that hinders the movements and deployment of the troops, also the Scottish mountains, where they carry out orientation exercises and movements of patrols.

Their training in other areas that leads them to share experiences in the training camps of Italy and the coasts of Spain should not be forgotten. The latter are frequently visited by the Dutch Royal Marines to carry out exercises with the Spanish marine infantry, a good example of this being seen in their deployment during the Tramontana 94 and Strong Resolve 98.

They also train in jungles and for this purpose they regularly travel to South American countries such as Belize and French Guyana where they share experiences with French, British or American troops. In Martinique and Guadeloupe for example, part of their training is carried out following that of French commandos.

Assault
The dual-cabin BV-206 Swedish vehicle, provides the Dutch Marines with the possibility of high mobility in the coastal area, it stands out for this high mobility and the capacity to transport up to fifteen men with their personal and collective equipment.

PERSONAL ARMAMENT OF THE DUTH MARINES

In 1994 the Dutch armed forces adopted the assault rifle C7 derived from the American model M16A2 and manufactured by DIEMACO in Canada. Rechambered to caliber 5.56x45 mm, this weapon stands out for incorporating magazines, manufactured in synthetic material, for thirty cartridges. It is also cheap to manufacture and resistant to military use. It lacks the top grip that has been replaced by a rail to which several night and day time scopes can be fixed, its total weight including its rapid targeting scope is of only 3.5 Kgs.
This scope corresponds to the British Wildcat manufactured by Hall and Watts Defence Optics. It is a third

generation scope that weighs around 350 grams to which 290 belong to the mount. It measures 160x72x55 mm, and includes a large frontal optic, that allows the observation of the target in adverse light conditions. It includes a reticule that facilitates both instinctive targeting and precision shots. This is contributed by the lenses that produce an enlargement of 3.4 diameters.
It also has in its favor the fact that the user has an ample view with respect to the target and it is sufficiently robust and air-tight to permit its use during amphibious disembarkments without suffering damage from blows or humidity.

Specific organization

All the operational units of the Royal Netherlands Marine Corps are grouped together under what is known as the GOUM (Group of Operational Units Marines). This is made up from 700 troops grouped in four Infantry battalions and organized into four companies: Three are of infantry and one is of support armament such as mortars, medium machine guns or anti-tank rocket launchers.

The 1st and 2nd battalions have their operational base at the Van Braam Houck-

Disembarkment

In November 1994 the beaches of Almería were the scene of a multinational amphibious disembarkment. This NATO exercise known as Tramontana included the participation of the Dutch Marines. These soldiers carried out their task with rifles lent by Spanish soldiers due to problems at French customs.

geest barracks in the city of Doom and constitute the main element of amphibious action. The third is a unit made up of reservists that can be quickly activated if the occasion so requires. The fourth is composed of both reservists and active personnel. These last total some 400 and are deployed in the Dutch Antilles and Aruba where they occupy installations at the Naval base of Parera and the barracks of Suffisant and Savaneta.

Doom houses the headquarters, the logistical battalions that groups together the diverse elements necessary to support the actions and deployment of the disembarked forces, and the combat support battalion. This last groups together the resources that support the actions of the

Position

During the combats that take place at the beachhead, light armament and equipment is usually used. This improves the mobility of the men in order to establish positions until they neutralize those of the opponent and progress little by little towards the interior.

infantry, be it with precise and punctual fire support, or with elements that allow them to reach previously determined points in actions undertaken. Its resources include heavy 120 mm mortars, portable launchers of light anti-aircraft Stinger missiles, and assault engineers.

For its part, the embarkation company is located at the Joost Douerlein barracks in the coastal city of Texel, and here all the assault vessels are concentrated, from small to the largest launches. The amphibious reconnaissance group, which is regarded as a special unit, is based at Den Helder.

To the former must be added the BBE (*Bijzondere Bijstands Eenheid*) that forms part of the marines, also at disposition of the Ministry of Justice for special actions carried out against terrorist movements or delinquent organized groups that could place public security at stake. Their usual tasks include assaults on oil platforms in the North Sea or practice with aircraft, trains or vessels.

International cooperation

In 1702, about 400 Dutch Marines took

part in the conquest of Gibraltar alongside British troops. Since then, they have maintained very good relations with the British, leading to the creation in the 70's of a joint amphibious force. This acts as a reinforced brigade and includes on some 5500 people. Its denomination is: UKNLPHIBGRU (UK/Netherlands Amphibious Task Group).

The Dutch contribution LF (Landing Force), consists of an Infantry battalion which is usually the 1st (1 MARNSBAT) and diverse elements of the battalions of logistical combat and support. These include a battery of heavy 120 mm mortars, a company of vessels for disembarking, a group specialized in mountain and arctic wars that usually trains in the difficult terrain of Norway, and an amphibian reconnaissance group. The latter groups together divers who reconnoiter beaches as a previous phase to amphibious attacks and can be deployed from submarines, parachutes or from small specialized boats.

Holland, as an active member of the

Messages
The rear of the Bv206 vehicle can be set up as a message emission and reception center, and has a capacity to house radio equipment, ciphering systems, display screens and an operations table.

NATO (North Atlantic Treaty Organization), has also participated since 1994 in the CAFMED (Combined Amphibious Force Mediterranean) and in the AMF (Allied Command Europe Mobile Force). This last contingent requires its components to mobilize elements in 48 hours in order to intervene rapidly where their presence may be required. It includes the 2nd Battalion (2MARNSBAT) that can act as an element assigned to the terrestrial component of the AMF (L).

Capacity and projection
These troops are ideal for missions in combat areas or pacification zones as a result of the resources that they possess and because of their individual prepara-

Communications
This soldier carries a rucksack fitted with radio equipment and its corresponding antenna. This system is valid both for transmissions on the ground and for ground-to-air at the beachhead.

Protection

From the bottom of the tactical jacket hangs the Kevlar helmet. The Dutch marines wear it when it is anticipated that actions of firing will take place, wearing the distinctive black cap when carrying out exercises or manoeuvers.

tion. This capacity, together with the political decision of the different Dutch governments of the last decades has led them to participate in all kinds of multinational organizations. At the same time, they have carried out actions to protect their own national interests.

Peacekeeping operations

One of the activities commended to the RNMC is their involvement in peace keeping tasks of the United Nations and these missions have increased over the last few years. If the Security Council of the United Nations so requires it, a force of interposition of battalion strength can be prepared and deployed in only one week and reinforced with 600-800 men. Once in the area of operation they may carry out a large variety of tasks that range from distributing humanitarian aid to

the use of force to ensure a cease-fire between opposing parties.

Throughout the 90's the Dutch Marines have participated in various peacekeeping operations. These began in 1991, with their deployment in Northern Iraq

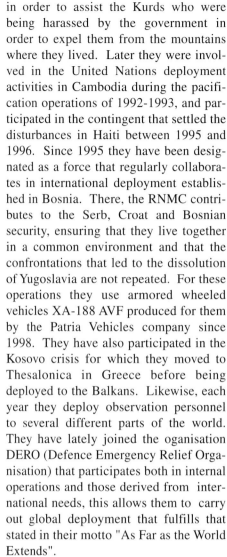

in order to assist the Kurds who were being harassed by the government in order to expel them from the mountains where they lived. Later they were involved in the United Nations deployment activities in Cambodia during the pacification operations of 1992-1993, and participated in the contingent that settled the disturbances in Haiti between 1995 and 1996. Since 1995 they have been designated as a force that regularly collaborates in international deployment established in Bosnia. There, the RNMC contributes to the Serb, Croat and Bosnian security, ensuring that they live together in a common environment and that the confrontations that led to the dissolution of Yugoslavia are not repeated. For these operations they use armored wheeled vehicles XA-188 AVF produced for them by the Patria Vehicles company since 1998. They have also participated in the Kosovo crisis for which they moved to Thesalonica in Greece before being deployed to the Balkans. Likewise, each year they deploy observation personnel to several different parts of the world. They have lately joined the oganisation DERO (Defence Emergency Relief Organisation) that participates both in internal operations and those derived from international needs, this allows them to carry out global deployment that fulfills that stated in their motto "As Far as the World Extends".

Amphibious forces

In order to deploy its own contingent and collaborate with the joint transport Brigade of Great Britain, a few years ago the Dutch Marine initiated an ambitious resourcing plan. This incorporated the joint collaboration with Spain under which it shared the design of a new type of ship LPD/ATS (Landing Platform Dock, Attack Transport Ship) that was built at the Royal Shelde shipyard.

Rotterdam

The amphibian assault vessel "Rotterdam" L800 handed over to the Marines in the spring of 1998, stands out, along with its Spanish twin for its noteable capacity for transport of men and material. Also for being able to locate helicopters and any other type of vehicle on the runway in the stern.

ROYAL NETHERLANDS MARINES

Combatants

The Dutch Marine Infantry soldier is a well trained, well equipped and veteran soldier. These qualities make him very useful for both amphibious missions and those of pacification where light and powerful units are needed.

This joint project has given a reduction in costs and of the time for manufacture that was initiated at the beginning of the 90s, and resulting from this the vessel Rotterdam L 800 was launched on the 25th January 1996.

Two years later on the 18th April 1998, it began its activity as a transport vessel, its noteable features being a capacity to mobilize 611 men and 33 combat tanks or 170 armored vehicles.

Its basic characteristics are very similar to those of the Spanish vessel "Galicia", it displaces 12,750 tons at full load, on its stern there is a runway from which three aircraft can operate simultaneously to the nine that may be stored in the hangar, and a floodable dock in which 4 launchers of LCM type can be located.

These characteristics have favored the planning of the construction of a second vessel in order to carry out aid and support tasks in those areas where a natural disaster has occurred. This second vessel

Helitransportation

The heavy Sea King Helicopters are capable of moving more than twenty men with their respective equipment and are also used by the Dutch Marines in joint exercises.

can be improved in some aspects such as improved command and control facilities and a larger runway, and could be ready in the year 2007. Its displacement will be of 20,000 tons and will receive the designation LHDC (Landing Helicopter Dock). In both of these vessels two multitube Goalkeeper artillery systems will be installed to guarantee defense against wave level anti-ship missiles.

As a complement to the larger units, a disembarkment fleet of launches is used which includes: Five LCU (Landing Craft Utility) MkIX that displace 200 tons and were completed in 1999, six 30 ton LCVP (Landing Craft Vehicles and Personnel) MkIII that are noted for incorporating a mount for the support of medium machine gun MG-42 and six LCVP MkII with a capacity for 35 men and a four wheeler Land Rover or a Snowcat tracked vehicle. The marine also has 22 Westland Lynx Helicopters used to give mobility to the troops by means of vertical assault. These are assigned to the more complex training that are often carried out by the SBS in one of the many oil platforms of the North

Sea. Their substitution is planned for 2007, and the new model will be the multipurpose NFH 90 of which 20 units have been ordered. On the Rotterdam it is usual to find AS-532 Cougar Mk2 Helicopters of the Dutch Air force. Each apparatus can carry up to 25 soldiers so that one rotation allows the transport of half a company to the beachhead. The latter, along with the capacity to act as a command ship or as a hospital vessel was proved during the Battle Griffin exercise that took place in 1998 in the north of Norway.

THE LYNX ASSAULT HELICOPTERS

From the flight deck of the Rotterdam, or from other vessels that are used jointly with the Dutch in manoeuvres or exercises, the British Westland Lynx helicopters can be used of which the Royal Netherlands Navy has about twenty Mk25 B, 27 A and 81 A. Due to its size, it is ideal to transport a squadron of eight men in the rear cabin or up to 900 Kgs of cargo, or to carry out various transports in its slings. It can also be used to infiltrate small commando groups that will be dropped to the water or on to the ground by means of a rope, to quickly deploy Stinger air to ground missile launchers or to provide mobility to mortar placements and avoid their destruction by the enemy's counter-batteries.

Its basic characteristics include an autonomy of 590 Kms, speed of 232 Kms/hr, high aerodynamic efficiency and excellent reliability. To this must be added the fact that it is a model which has been on the market for many years and has undergone continuous renewal. Its configuration with fixed undercarriage and shock absorbers allows it to land in many types of location.

If necessary, lateral gun mountings can be installed to carry different models of light weapons or rocket launchers to support the ground troops.

Italy maintains Armed Forces of a notably large size to which it dedicates a large proportion of the national budget. By doing this, it guarantees operational status as well as the supply of all types of modern equipment. Given the geo-strategic situation and great length of the Italian coastline, its naval and amphibious resources must be deployed in such a manner as to permit intervention in the most varied of scenarios. The San Marco group represents the principal element of men and resources that can be deployed directly to a beach-head or transferred by other means, wherever the need may arise.

Tradition, evolution and adaptation

The origins of this amphibious element date back to August 1713, the year in which King Vittorio Amadeo II of Sicily ordered the creation of the first Regiment of Sardinia. This Regiment under the name of La Marina, opposed the French between the years 1792 to 1796 as a consequence of the movements of expansion that France maintained on various European frontiers.

History full of interventions

It was at the beginning of 1815 when this unit grew to the status of brigade, and

Counter-armor

In order to guarantee a capacity for neutralization of targets of special importance, German launchers Panzerfaust III are employed that fire grenades of various types permitting opposition to armored casemates as well as armored vehicles.

this was maintained until 1845, year in which its missions were transferred to the Real Navi battalion that participated in the first Italian war of independence and was dissolved in 1851. In the following decade, under the command of Cavour, the battalion was reactivated under the title of Fanteria Real Marina. It was assigned the mission of protecting of arsenals, acting as an element of disembarking and defending maritime installations, and amongst its actions figures the battle of Lissa fought against the Austrians and also the disturbances of 1866 in Palermo.

In 1879, it was deployed in Tunis to fight against the guerillas that were harassing the Italians; in 1889 they acted on the island of Crete, in 1890 they were involved in the combats which stopped the disturbances of the Boxers in Peking and, in 1911, were deployed to Tripoli (Libya). During the World War of 1914, during which more men were required to fight in

Rifle

The basic arm of the Italian marine infantry is the assault rifle Beretta AR-70/90. This arm fires cartridges of .223 Remington of which 30 are located in the magazine.

Support

The equipping of the sections of arms support include medium machine guns MG-42/58, modified to incorporate a nocturnal optical-electronic sight that permits use both day and night.

the trenches, its organization was integrated into the navy, however it was not until 17th March 1919 that the decree constituting the San Marco was promulgated.

In 1925, a group of 300 of its members were formed into a group that was sent to China to protect the legations and concessions of Italy during the civil war, remaining in that territory until 1943. In 1936, they landed in Ethiopia and did the same in Albania three years afterwards.

During the Second World War the

Circulation

The Iveco VM-90 vehicles are light lorries of high tactical mobility that can transfer a patrol and incorporate a mount for fixing the potent and precise medium machine gun M-2 of .50 caliber Browning.

entity was increased to undertake requirements of several fronts in the Mediterranean, Dalmatia, Montenegro, and in North Africa and Greece.

As a result of the Italian surrender to the Allies and the change of side, a reconstitution of San Marco was carried out and

it fought alongside the 13th British Corps on the Cassino front, at los Abruzzos and on the Adriatic coast. A period of uncertainty followed the cessation of hostilities that terminated in 1965 with its formation as a battalion that lasted until 1999 when it was decided to enlarge the entity to that of

ITALIAN SAN MARCO GROUP

Navigation

The Italian marine infantry includes in its organization personal prepared for the manipulation of rapid assault vessels, men that wear dry suits that protect them from the inclemencies derived from the rapid movements on the surface of the water.

a Brigade, with increases in both its human and material resources.

In 1982, it was deployed in Beirut (Lebanon), as part of a Multinational Peace Force. There it suffered a number of losses amongst its members as the result of attacks by Shi'ite guerillas who launched a grenade against one of the Italian all-terrain vehicles. This mission continued until 1984 and included the deployment of a contingent of some three hundred men. Later, other activities were carried out such as an element of interposition in places as far apart as Somalia, the former Yugoslavia and Albania, where a contingent was deployed at the end of the 90's.

Reaggrupamento Anfibio San Marco

This is the denomination that is given to the Italian amphibious component at the present time, and its commander is a captain of the navy. This Group is integrated into the structure of the Italian Terza Divisione Navale de la Marina Militare whose commander is a rear-admiral. It has the status of a brigade and is configured with a

command and headquarters structure, and three units of battalion level: the logistic group, the training group, and the San Marco battalion that has some 2,000 men. This number is in the process of being increased in order to complete the force anticipated under the last organization, which envisages the configuration of an entity formed of two combat battalions plus appropriate support.

The command and headquarters deal with which the planning and control of training and of the planning of operations.

The logistic group is given the task of providing diverse types of support in administration, logistics and infrastructure via the services of Transport, Logistic-Administrative, Medical and General. The training group, located on the small island of Pedagne, has the task of carrying out the basic and advanced formation of all personnel and of preparing those destined for tasks related to the security of the fixed installations of the Marina Militare: this training being assigned to the Escuela de Fusileros de Marina, and to the Escuela de Servicios de Defensa de Instalaciones to which must be added the command that coordinates the supervision of both.

With respect to San Marco, with barracks in the base of Brindisi, this constitutes the operative amphibious element of the group and it is expected that it will exceed, in itself, some 2,000 men. Its current organization includes a unit of command and services, and assault companies, of transport and support armaments. The command unit includes elements of reconnaissance, medical, logistical, com-

Ships

The L 9894 San Giusto is the most modern and capable of the three ships of their type that the Italian Marine Militare has available to it. This capacity will be increased within a few years with the with which addition of a larger and improved vessel.

SUB-RIFLE BERETTA M-12

The Italian company Pietro Beretta, having its main production plant in Gardone Val Trompia (Brescia), has produced the sub-rifle Model 12 since the early 1960's. This weapon is outstanding for its ergonometric design and for its reliability. It is exported to ten countries and used by specialized groups such as the Special Weapons and Tactics (SWAT) of the Los Angeles Police. The M12 stands out for its weight of 3 kilograms, including a metal stock that folds over the right side, includes a forward pistol grip that permits a better grip and protected forward and rear sights. Furthermore, the safety lever is located in the rear grip so that accidental firing is avoided when the weapon is not being used.

The breech block is for cartridges of 9x19 millimeters Parabellum and is capable of firing magazines of 20, 32 or 40 cartridges at a rate of 550 rounds per minute All the examples used by the San Marcos have been provided with a forward fitting that permits location of a "Laser Products" powerful torch that easily illuminates the area in which the rifle is pointed and thus facilitates a greater efficiency in firing.

munications and fire control (FSSC).

The assault companies are formed into a command section, three of infantry, one of transport and one of armaments, in which some two hundred infantry are distributed. Also included are two very specialist elements known as the DOA (Demolitori Ostacoli Antisbarco) and the RECON (Nuclei di Rigognitori). The arms support companies are configured into mortar and missile sections, with anti-tank and anti-aircraft launchers of portable type.

The Reaggruppamento San Marco forms part of the Italian Rapid Intervention Force (FIR) and is integrated into multi-national defensive organizations such as European Rapid Operative Force (EURO-FOR), the European Maritime Force (EROMARFOR), the The Combined Amphibious Force of the Mediterranean (CAFMED) and the Spanish-Italian Amp-

hibious Force (SIAF) that, every two years, assigns a rotating command between both countries. Within its own military naval organization part of the Terza Divisione Navale is organized in which are included landing vessels and some rapid patrol boats of Sparviero type, currently in the process of being retired from service. Command belongs to the rear-admiral COMFORANF who directs the naval, aerial and landing elements.

Operational qualification

The missions assigned to this type of amphibious force, such as spearheading attack on a beach in hostile territory with large attrition during the advance, decides the type of preparation of its components.

ITALIAN SAN MARCO GROUP

These are trained in such fields as infiltration, survival, and the use of the most varied of armaments.

The formation of components

The greatest part of the actual components of command derives from the navy, contrary to that which applied a few years ago when a good part came from the Army. The officers have received special military training and including that derived from participation in specialized courses such as that of infiltation taught in Varignano.

Once assigned to a battalion they pass through intensive and specific training, for two months, in the Infantry School and this includes preparation in diverse areas: terrestrial combat, navigation in vessels, scaling of cliffs, collaboration with helicopters, landing in boats, amphibious assault, etc., that will permit them to adapt to their later postings as commanders of elements of operations.

Administrative disembarking
These amphibious assault ships include a portal on the port side that permits the connection between holds and the quay where the ship is tied up thus permitting the rapid discharge of men and light vehicles.

For their part, the troops that have passed previously through the recruiting centers of La Spezia and Tarento to receive initial training in the new tasks that they will undertake in the military structure, follow specific and intensive training. This includes a first cycle of eight weeks that prepares soldiers for individual combat and a second cycle to which access is given only to the most prepared. This complementary training prepares them for working within patrols and sections, and also includes specialization such as infiltration, handling of mortars, serving grenade launchers, marksmanship, explorers, missile experts, radiotelegraph operators, and others.

At the end of this period of training of five months, the best prepared are posted to the more active units and become part of the elite Italian amphibious force. Their instruction will continue with all types of national and international exercises that improve the personal and professional qualification of those participating, whatever the rank and operative destination of these.

Equipment of the highest level

The *maró,* a name that has been given to the Italian marine infantry by the armed forces of their country, are provided with

MILAN
The French anti-armor system MILAN consists of light launchers and containers where the missiles are stored. It is capable of reaching targets located at between 25 and 2,000 meters. Its wire homing device permits a high ratio of impact.

varied and modern personal equipment with complements of collective use, that includes areas such as uniforms, individual and support armaments, and combat elements.

Within the first of these is found the mimetic field uniform, in tones of green and brown, that stands out for its variety of colors that degrade notably with washing, so that there is a considerable difference the appearance of a new one compared to one that which has been used for some time. As a complement the black beret used in barracks and during navigation, the modern tactical jacket of national design, the holster for a pistol corresponding to the Bianchi UM-84 model, the mixed leather boots used in all types of combat activities together with elements of personal protection that include anti-flack jackets as well as Kevlar helmets manufactured in Cassoni, including a model that incorporates a shielded peak in front for facial protection.

Personal equipment also includes the uniforms and face masks that permit combat in areas contaminated with aggressive elements NBQ (Nuclear, Bacteriological or Chemical). The goggles

Assault
The three ships of type San Marco incorporate a floodable dock in the stern that can accommodate two launches of type LCM with heavy equipment that they transport from this point up to the beachhead. Two additional LCM are transported in an accompanying area.

Equipment
The high quality equipment of the **maró**, *ranges from tactical jackets to Kevlar helmets. In combat these Italian infantry respond with a high level of initiative in the tasks assigned to them by their command and represent an eminently offensive force.*

that protect from dust, the harnesses for rappel that facilitates circulation in rough terrain and the aqua-diving equipment includes neoprene suits, dry suits for immersion in small depths, bottles and all necessary complementary items.

The armament used by the Italians is modern, varied and stands out for its adaptation for the assigned mission. Each soldier is provided with an assault rifle Beretta SC70/90 with breech block for firing cartridges of caliber 5.56x45 mm and configured with a stock that folds to one side. The officers carry a semi-automatic pistol Beretta 92FS with a magazine for 15 rounds of caliber 9x19 mm Parabellum, whilst for special missions the sub-rifles Beretta M12 and Heckler und Köck MP5, of the same caliber as the above, are particularly useful. Associated with these Sure-

Infiltration

The heavy helicopters SH-3D Sea King of the Marina Militare are employed for operations of aerial assault of the first troops that must consolidate strategic locations in the area selected for the amphibious deployment.

Fire torches are used to facilitate nocturnal targeting in that they project a strong focus of light over targets.

More specific are the bolt operated Winchester shot guns, firing cartridges of caliber 12/70, SC70/90 rifles adapted for marksmanship and as complementary support in actions, day and night optical sco-

Communications

The deployment of an amphibious force at a hostile point far away from the operative base requires the men to carry a varied collection of communication equipment that permits the maintenance of links between the units deployed , at the same time serving to contact the command headquarters.

pes and the SMAL (Stabilimento Militare Armi Leggere) single firing grenade launchers of 40 mm. In situations where maximum precision is required a combination of British and United States rifles are used. Amongst the first of these the Accuracy

AW of 7.62 mm and the AWM Super Magnum stand out, firing the powerful .338 Lapua Magnum. Ideal for those missions requiring firing over large distances and against protected targets are the McMillan 12.70x99mm (.50 Browning)

caliber supplied by the United States.

The same caliber applies to the heavy machine guns Browning and Springfield M-2 which are employed using mounts on various types of vehicles or from a mobile tripod. In the segment of light machine guns the durable Minimi made by the FN Herstal company are available firing belted ammunition of 5.5. In the medium group are found MG-42/59 of German origin but manufactured in Italy under license, weapon firing belts of 7.62 mm and which have been adapted with a support to fix an optical-electronic night scope. Likewise, the SMAL company has developed a conversion unit that, with a new barrel and a modified breech, permits the firing of cartridges of 5.56.

Against targets of greater resistance disposable rocket launchers C-90C of the Spanish company Instalaza are used as also are launchers of bivalent grenades Dynamit Nobel Panzerfaust 3 that are of German origin and have a maximum range of 500 meters. As a complement to the above, an extensive range of systems are deployed including: the anti-tank missile

ARMORED VCC-1 CAMILLINO

In order to improve the armoring of the tracked M-113 of the United States, which the Italians produce under license in the factory of OTOBREDA, the Servizio Tecnico della Motorizzazione of the Italian army initiated transformation studies to provide a more efficient model. This resulted in a vehicle that was produced until 1982 and that is notable for having improved ballistic protection that combines steel and aluminum, even in the walls of the rear part combined with a certain amount of inclination that favors its resistance to impact. It incorporates observation windows and slits for guns in the compart-

ment for the transport of infantry and confides self defense to a turret with heavy machine gun M-2 that also benefits from a certain amount of lateral protection. As a result of these modifications, to which must be added large fuel tanks located in the rear, the VCC-1 weighs 11.6 tons, measures 5.4 meters, is capable of moving at 64.4 kilometers per hour and its autonomy is of some 550 kilometers. Some examples have been provided with an Israeli EAAK packet consisting of additional armoring plates.

launchers Euromissile MILAN with a Galileo thermic scope; the French medium mortar MO-81-61 L of 81 mm of the Thompson Brand company that can fire grenades at targets at a range of 6 km.; the heavy mortars MO-120-60 of 120 mm that, in order to obtain greater tactical mobility, are found in the rear of the armored tracked vehicle M-106; and the Stinger anti-aircraft missile launchers of United States origin.

Other elements to be assigned include spectacle-binoculars for night vision, optical-electronic night scopes made by the companies Aeritalia SpA and Officine Galileo SpA, Laser telemeters LP7,

Missile
The anti-aircraft defense of the elements deployed to the beachhead is assigned to patrols with Stinger light missile launchers, weapons of a type known as "fire and forget" that automatically lock onto the target.

Amphibious
The LVTP-7 are tracked amphibious vehicles of United States origin that can navigate on the surface thanks to the hydro-jets propulsion units and that have a capacity, in its interior, for some twenty fully equipped soldiers. These men can advance to the point of disembarking behind the protection of the armor.

communications equipment of the United States AN/PRC-77 family and the Israeli Tadirán, with capacity for anti-interference, portable equipment for telephone links via satellite or semi-rigid vessels and kayaks. To provide mobility during deployments and exercises they use; light all-terrain vehicles Land Rover, light lorries Iveco VM-90 which include a mount for the M-2 on their upper part, medium lorries ACM-80 and heavy ACP-80, vehicles and machinery for engineers and intendancy and armored tracked

Satellite
Today, the troops need to be in constant contact with their superiors that can be located at hundreds or thousands of miles or kilometers from where the action is taking place. For these links they need systems that benefit from the global coverage of diverse satellites in geo-stationary orbit.

three medium helicopters can operate simultaneously and a loading capacity amounting to 350 infantry and 1,000 tons of diverse material that can be stored in the holds and storage areas. The holds can be reached either via a lateral door that connects directly to the quay or via another at the front that facilitates access to the floodable dock in which can be situated, simultaneously, two vessels of LCM (Landing Craft Medium) type. Their maximum speed is 20 knots and they can travel, without refueling, a distance of 7,500 nautical miles navigating at a speed of 16.

The Luigi Einaud, which at present is only at the design stage, has been conceived as a vessel of 22,500 tons that is outstanding for its large extended deck of on which may be located helicopters as well as vertical take-off aircraft such as Harriers, for which a sky jump ramp is located at the bow. It is conceived to give mobility to a force of some 600 infantry and carry a load of 28 combat tanks or 50 lorries of various types. It will also count on a floodable dock in the poop from which it is envisaged that LCM's will be deployed as well as air cushioned vehicles of type LCAC (Landing Craft Air Cushion).

At this time, the support function that represents the above is confided to the aircraft carrier C 551 Giuseppe Garibaldi that can transport, combining deck and hold, some twenty aircraft, whether these be medium assault helicopters or logistical transport SH Sea King, that will be

replaced by new EH-101 in a few years, or light assault helicopters and near fire support AB-212 or again vertical take-off aircraft of type Harrier AV-8B Plus. These will be used to transport men and material to the beach-head in order to destroy the defenses established by the enemy and to establish the necessary air superiority in the action area.

Smaller, but of vital importance in certain amphibious actions, are two launches of type Pedretti that are used to transport COMSUBIN assault divers, assigned to the beaches where landing is proposed, fourteen launches LCM of United States or Italian origin, displacing some sixty tons and capable of transporting a combat tank or a hundred men, and sixteen vessels LCVP (Landing Craft Vehicles and Personnel) of 14.6 tons and capacity for 40 totally equipped persons.

vehicles VCC-1 Camillino for the transport of personal. To this list must be added the versatile tracked amphibious transport LVTP-7 that can navigate in water and has a capacity to transport some twenty marine infantry behind the protection of its armoring.

Amphibious movements.

The San Marco group can displace to the intervention point thanks to naval support that is given by the Marina Miltare and includes vessels as well as helicopters. In the first group are to be found modern LPD (Landing Platform Dock), of the San Giorgio type, that include the L 9892 of the same name, the L 9893 named San Marco and the L 9894 San Giusto. All will be complemented by the L 552 Luigi Einaudi that will commence construction in the year 2000 for entry into service seven years later.

The first two ships have a displacement of 7,600 tons that is increased to 8,000 in the case of the third. They were placed into service in 1987, 1988 and 1994 thanks to a financing from budgets of the Ministries of Defense and Civil Protection. Amongst their most significant features figure: a crew of 160 officers and marines, a flight deck of 100 meters length and 20.5 width from which

Light support
The Belgian light machine gun Minimi has been chosen by the San Marco battalion and has been incorporated at patrol level. With them they obtain precise and consistent support fire over locations that present most resistance to their own advance.

The French army (Armée de Terre) maintains, amongst its various components, the "Inspection des Troupes de Marine", that is stationed in the cuartel of Caseme de Reuilly with a Divisional general acting as commander of these troops. Their utilization covers some dozen locations in French territory with elements located in Africa as well as Central America, supporting the political policies of the Government in Paris.

Used throught the world

The appearance of this type of specialized troops dates from the XVII century, with the obligation to count on forces that could defend territories that the

Vehicles

For their transport a combination of Peugeot P4 all terrain and lorries of medium and large tonnage are used, a large part of these also being manufactured by Peugeot. These vehicles are easily transported by sea up to the point of utilization.

French were conquering overseas. In 1622 Cardenal Richelieu created the hundred marine companies that were transformed into Marine regiments, putting them in charge of, at the end of the century, the defense of the large ports of Brest, Rochefort and Toulon, with their artillery pieces, and the Canadian cam-

Marksmen

For carrying out its missions such as an amphibious force and for global intervention, means of surgical exactness are required to achieve objectives with great precision, figuring among these the precise FR-F2 of 7.62x51 millimeter caliber.

paign. In the middle of the XVIII century the recruitment of indigenous troops for incorporation into these units began and amongst these were found the Cipayes aux Indes of 1750 or the Laptots de Gorée, of Senegal. Under King Luis XVI eight regiments served to defend ports and other locations overseas. All of these were transformed during the French revolution into infantry regiments.

In 1822 Louis Philippe, promoted the formation of the 1st and 2nd Marine regiments, whose number increased as a result of colonial interests, so that in 1822 four infantry and one artillery regiment existed. Within these 120 companies and 27 artillery batteries were grouped, which provides an idea of their large military potential. Their dispersal covered Africa, the Baltics, Crimea, the Far East and Mexico, and among their actions figures the landing at Bazeiller on 31 August 1870, when 2,600 men lost their lives.

With the arrival of the twentieth century, the "Troupes de Marine" were involved in the first and second world wars, and they were located during these two wars in Morocco, where they fought in the Riff. Later came the tragic events of

Parachutists
The French "Troupes de Marine" includes various parachutist regiments that specialize in aerial assault operations, whether these be via air launches or in air transport operations depending on medium sized helicopters.

Dien Bien Phu of Vietnam in 1954, their posting in Algeria, the battles in Indochina, interventions to calm unrest in numerous colonies and displacement, without rest, where it was necessary. In 1990, on the occasion of the invasion of Kuwait by Iraq, it was decided to send some 3,500 marine infantry, and these fought the Iraqi forces with combat vehicles, artillery pieces and infantry transport vehicles.

More recent events are: the position in Krajina in 1992, in order to serve as an element of interposition before the aggressive events that threatened the former Yugoslavia; the operation to take the airport of Sarajevo and permit the arrival of humanitarian aid; an intervention in Somalia in mid 1993; the assault of Vrbanja of 1995, and the integration into the Implementation Force (IFOR) of NATO. In 1996 and 1997 they were sent

Transport
The L 9030 "Champlan" is a ship for transport of vehicles and logistical elements and heads a class of five units that are known by the generic term of BATRAL. Its displacement is 1,300 Tons with full load.

Combat
Wheeled combat vehicles that are used by the "Troupes de Marine" include these AMX-10RC that stand out for their good tactical mobility, notable protection with a supplementary kit and a high firing capacity, using a low pressure gun of 105 millimeters.

Fire power
The heavy type M-2 machine gun firing belted munitions of 12.7x90 millimeter caliber, is able to target objectives with notable precision at a range of 1,500 meters and easily penetrate light armor.

to the Central African Republic, and have also taken part in "Operation Turquesa" in Rwanda and in the recent operations in Albania.

Many units

Some 30,000 personnel form the marine infantry of the French army including 2,000 officers and 6,000 non commissioned officers. They are dispersed in such a manner that 75 % are located in France with the rest in garrisons of other countries.

Recruits may choose between seven specialties in which to serve: that of the infantry in which men have to be capable of marching 100 kilometers in 24 hours; the specialist aereotransportation group, specializing in aerial infiltration by aircraft and helicopters, integrating parachutists qualified to leap from great heights such as HALO (High Altitude, Low Opening) and HAHO (High Altitude, High Opening); the heavy armored group that is entrusted with managing the diverse types of armored vehicles supporting group movements; the commando group that carry out high risk special missions that require a higher level of prepa-

ration than normal; the amphibious group, that exploits the capability for landing in coastal areas; the communications group that manages equipment to guarantee links under any circumstance and the artillery, to arrange the make up and supply of armaments and ammunition.

The organization continues with locations in French territory and in several ex colonies. In the first of these is found the 9° Division d'Infantarie de Marine (DiMa) consisting of some 7,500 personnel, and this is included within the Rapid Action Force, which possesses on half a million armored vehicles and seven hundred anti-tank systems, and divides its forces between the 1° Régiment d'Infanterie de Marine (RIMa) of Angoulème acting as an explorer force, the 2° RIMa of Mans, the 3° RIMa of Vannes, the Régiment d'Infanterie of Chars de Marine (RICMa), the 11° Régiment d'Artillerie de Marine (RAMa), and the 9° Régiment de Commandement et de Soutien (RCS) entrusted with logistical tasks.

The aerotransportation regiment Régiment Parachutiste d'Infanterie de Marine (RPIMa) composing of units 1, 3, 6 and 8 enjoys independent status and the first of these carries out very varied missions within special operations. To the above must be added the 4° RIMa of Fréjus and the motorized 21° RIMa; the 1° and 3° RAMa's with autopropulsion means, and the Régiment de Marche du Tchad (RMT).

The 9° and 33° RIMa of Guyana and Marinique are based In Central America as also the 41° "Bataillon d'Infanterie de Marine" (BIMa) of Guadalupe. In Africa is the 2° RPIMa and the 53° "Bataillon de Commandement et de Soutien" (BCS) located in Madagascar, the 5° "Regiment inter Armes d'Outre-Mer" (RIAOM) and the 10° BCS in Djibouti, the 6° BIMa in Gabon that supports the "Centre d'Entrai-

AS-532 COUGAR HELICOPTERS

The French army operates, via the ALAT, diverse medium transport helicopters of the "Puma" family and its current variant "Cougar" that incorporates certain modifications to increase its competitiveness. Of these is the AS-532 that carries the weight of transport operations of troops, commandos and loads in the most varied of scenarios, for which reason it is usual that these apparatus take off from the landing platforms of amphibious vessels to support whatever amphibious assault operation whether this be in the first wave of aerial transport or in the subsequent logistical movements. Its large and lengthy cabin permits the transport of up to twenty soldiers with their equipment in two long seats located in a central position, men can reach the interior by means of two lateral doors. Its two high powered Turbomeca Makila turbines provide high agility and potential, its outstanding feature being the capability of flying with an internal load, including fuel, that exceds 4.5 tons.

nemaint Commando" (CEC FOGA); the 23ª BIMa at Cabo Verde and the 43° BIMa in the Ivory Coast. Likewise the "Regiment d'Infanterie de Marine du Pacifique Novelle-Caédonie" (RIMaP) in New Caledonia and in Polynesia, the battalion infantry body of the above mentioned being some 500 men and of the regiments some 800.

The missions assigned to the above units, constituting an element highly significant as a body within the French army, includes the defense of continental territory, the reinforcement of NATO resources in Europe in order to face any kind of threat, the constitution of a very mobile body capable of rapid transfer in order to face any type of crisis and to form garrisons in areas and ex colonies of diverse interests of a political or economic nature.

High dissuasive level

The French "Troupes de Marine" is a highly mobile body with a high capacity for transfer wherever French interests

Armor

The Renault VAB are an armored class of vehicles with double axle and all wheel drive that serve to give mobility to some ten men and transport them, under the protection of its cabins, up to the point at which they will carry out their intervention, also used in patrols.

may lie, a quality that was demonstrated during the Gulf War in Kuwait and Iraq. To this capacity must be added its distribution throughout the world that facilitates rapid location wherever necessary in order to resolve a local crisis, whether as a result of the geopolitical requirements of France or those deriving from its international commitments.

Capacity for combat

The personnel forming the troops of the French Marine combine uniforms of traditional green with more modern

Mechanical mules

The parachute regiments of the "Troupes de Marine" use Fardier vehicles manufactured by Lohr to move small logistical loads, such as mortars and their supports. Thanks to these, emplacements can be changed rapidly.

mimetic uniforms that incorporate Gore-Tex fibers to improve impermeability and transpiration, the use of the red or black beret being usual where the activity is not specifically that of combat. The harnes-

Light armament

The French Marine infantry is assigned, as elements of support, Belgian Minim light machine guns modified with a shortened barrel so that it can be transported more easily. These arms fire belted .223 Remington munitions.

sing is based on a belt and two straps that support and serve to carry diverse personal equipment such as knives, torches or grenades, hanging from the first of these a spade, holders for magazines, or a holster for a pistol; tactical jackets are also available as also are suits for wearing in areas where NBQ (Nuclear, Bacteriological and Chemical) agents have been disseminated and these are associated with gas masks with lateral filter cartridges and PR4G communication equipment that incorporates agile change of frequency.

Personal protection is based on the use of various types of helmet amongst which the most significant is of Kevlar following the lines of the American M1 and including over its surface the same camouflage material as the uniform, complementing the former with a thick and heavy flack-

Launching

The transport aircraft of the French "Armée de l'Air", particularly the C-130 Hercules and Transall, permit the carrying of men and material wherever necessary in order to launch them over land, this facility being available to all the parachute regiments.

proof jacket that features large pockets in the front and back in which plates capable of resisting light armaments and projectiles may be placed.

Of the armaments used by these forces the most important is the semi-automatic pistol configured for individual use that may be a copy of the Beretta 02 made in France, or an older model, as also the FAMAS assault rifle, of compact design of whose the long top barrel, used for aiming and carrying, is an outstanding feature. The special units also use German sub rifles Heckler und Köck MP5 in its silenced version SD, sub rifles Mini Uzi and assault rifles M16 using 5.56 ammunition normalized by NATO for this type of armament.

For collective use various precision rifles are used, all activated by means of a bolt, amongst which may be found the FR-F2 of .308 Winchester and the Hecate, McMillan M-87R and Barrett of

12.7x99 (.50 Browning), the first three of these being activated by bolt and the last being of semi-automatic type. The cartridge of the .50 is used by the heavy M2 HB machine guns that are used from vehicle mounts as well as terrestrial supports, armaments that complement the light machine gun Minimi Para of 5.56 and the French medium machine guns AAT 52 and Belgian MAG, and as complementary armaments an ample selection is used, ranging from grenades for personal use, through to double barrel shotguns of 12/70 caliber used in jungle locations.

Fire support is provided by a different type of mortars, using those of 60mm of South African origin, of 81 mm that are usually transported by mechanical Fardier Lohr mules so that they can be moved with greater mobility, and the heavy Brandt of 120 mm that requires a towed carriage. On counter attack mis-

SELF-PROPELLED HOWITZER AUF-1 CGT

This artillery piece is a updated version of that which commenced production in 1977 and consists of a lightened chassis of the AMX-30 tank on which an armored turret has been mounted with an artillery piece of 155 mm. Three men travel in its interior, to whom must be added the driver, who is entrusted with managing fire support and counting with the assistance of an automatic magazine that permits the rapid movement of the 155 mm munitions, obtaining very high rates of fire of up to 6 rounds in 45 seconds. Outstanding features of this piece is that it has a combat weight of 42 tons that restricts its mobility in transfers by land or in disembarking launches, that the motor of 720 horsepower enables it to overcome obstacles of vertical heights of over a meter and trenches of two meters, and due to its length of barrel can target distances up to 29 kilometers away. As a secondary armament a medium machine gun of 7.62 caliber is used as an element of self defense against aerial attack and a heavy machine gun of 12.7 caliber serves to fight terrestrial objectives.

Recently a process of updating has been carried out to provide an auxiliary unit with greater capacity and global positioning systems permitting a more precise navigation.

sions 89 mm LRAC rocket launchers and Apilas of disposable type are complemented by short range Eryx missiles and medium range wire guided MILAN, the latter using the thermic chamber Mira that permits night firing; also assigned are short range HOT missiles mounted on VAB vehicles.

Anti-aircraft self-defense is confided to monotube guns of 20mm that may be mounted on the bodies of two axle Renault TRM-1000 lorries and to portable launchers of light type using short range missiles Matra Mistral receiving data from targets captured by Samantha radar associated with their emplacement, whilst for support by artillery fire recourse is made to towed and self propelled items that include BF-50, TRF 1 and GCT AUF1. In order to direct fire the Atila system is installed on vehicles.

For combat actions a large selection of wheel driven armored vehicles are used, including M11 "Ultrav" associated with reconnaissance missions, AML in its variant with mortar of 60 mm as well as low pressure canon of 90, VAB for transport of troops that are also used for support missions equipped with canons of 20 mm or with radar RATAC for terrestrial vigilance, Sagaie ERC-90 6x6 with a 90 mm piece and the powerful AMX-10RC provided with a canon of 105 mm fitted with improved armoring. The infantry combat units use the AMX-10P crawler mounted vehicles and the AOV variant for artillery observation and some medium combat vehicles AMX-30 B.

For those actions requiring rapid movements, and in order to count on an adequate level of complementary fire potential, four wheeled motorcycles with all wheel drive are used, assault buggies armed with medium and heavy machine guns, all terrain Peugot P4 light vehicles equipped with two anchorages to fit AA-52 machine guns and light Acmat VLRA lorries on which are located diverse types of armaments. In their displacement in rivers and lakes the Zodiac pneumatic launches with capacity for 6 people are very useful as also are the patrol boats with rigid hull.

Aerial and naval assault

The French Marine Nationale contributes various naval units to the displacement capacity of its "Troupes de Marine". In this group may be found the LPD (Landing Platform Dock) L 9077 "Bougainville" that has a capacity to move 500 soldiers and a 1,180 ton load, the LSD (Landing Ship Dock) L 9011 "Foudre" and l 9012 "Siroco" that displace 17,200 tons, a feature of which are the three flight decks that permit simultaneous operation of four helicopters, and the LSD L 9021 "Ougaran" and L 9022 "Orange" that are used principally to transport large quantities of armored and wheeled vehicles up to beach bridgeheads. Towards the middle of the first decade of the 21st century it is anticipated that two new LSD/LPD, similar to the existing "Foudre" class, will be placed

Assault

The L 9011 "Foudre" is a modern amphibious assault ship whose outstanding features include the installations that permit the landing of transport helicopters and the floodable dock, qualities much appreciated when mobility has to be provided to an amphibious contingent.

into service in order to reinforce the fleet and replace the training ship "Jeanne d'Arc".

In support of the above mentioned five, LST's are available that serve to give mobility to a dozen vehicles and which are also located in overseas bases such as New Caledonia and French Guyana. Movement between transport ships and beaches is carried out by three large launches type "Edic" 700 of 736 tons, 22 CTM (Chalands de Transport de Matériel) launches with a maximum military load capacity of 90 tons, two LCM-6 and two CDIC destined for the transport of infantry.

When the occasion so requires, transport helicopters of both the army and navy may be used, the most important of the former being the ASD-332 "Super Puma" of ALAT and of the latter the Aerospatiale SA 321 G "Super Frelon"

Disembarking

For landing launches, amphibious elements may be deployed on those bridge-heads on the coast or beach that have the necessary gradient to permit the advance of men and vehicles. This facility permits deployment all over the world.

with a capacity for twenty-seven passengers or the SA 365F "Dauphin 2" that can be used to insert small groups of commandos. Also, the capacity for transport of the C-130 "Hercules" and "Transail" of l'Armee de l'Air are usually employed to move troops during aerial assault and parachute launches.

The peculiar political situation that has prevailed in the second half of the twentieth century in the countries of Central and South America has given rise to the maintenance of dictatorial governments managed by the military or into a profusion of revolutionary politics that has affected certain countries. These movements to install serious and firm governmental institutions has resulted in the maintenance of very strong military structures, particularly so if we take into account the low economic development of the area that has been used, in some cases, as an element of repression against the civil population or as an organization to guarantee the rule of the will of a minority.

Within these military elements many marine infantry units have been established that have seen adaptation of their organizations, resources and characteristics to

Operatives
The Chilean Marine infantry constitutes a highly capacitated and trained nucleus to operate under the most difficult conditions. These troops are notable for their modern equipment high quality that includes the United States Colt M16 of 5.56 caliber.

suit the background in which they had to carry out their mission, differing between those that have enormous coastlines to defend and those nations that employ these specialized forces to patrol rivers in large jungle areas.

Marine infantry of the south
The southern area of the continent has been the scene of certain geostrategic rivalry between Argentina and Chile, differences that have given rise to certain minor

Transport
The Argentine units have French wheeled armored vehicles Panhard VCR assigned to them for their deployment of which there are examples with mounts for 20 millimeter guns that can be used against both terrestrial and aerial targets.

military skirmishes. That which has been significant has been the claim maintained by the Argentineans concerning sove-

Training
The Chilean Marine infantry is noted for its level of training and modern equipment, of particular importance amongst the latter being the Zodiac pneumatic launches that are propelled by two powerful outboard motors.

reignty over the Falkland Islands that are close to their continental territory but belong to the United Kingdom.

Amphibious assault
This historic claim led the military of the last Argentine dictatorship to program the reconquering of the islands by means of a military operation that was initiated on the 2nd of April 1982 and that had as its principal focus elements of the 1st. Infantry Battalion of the Marine Infantry and of the Amphibious Command Group, unit that, in the initial combats, lost its leader Captain Guichino. Its first action, carried out in an impeccable manner and without causing losses amongst the British forces, demonstrated their preparation and possibilities for employment, although eventually they

Amphibious units
The Chilean LST of "Maipo" type are used to transfer men and material up to the point at which an amphibious assault is taking place, carrying out the deployment to the coast by means of pneumatic boats or taking the vessel up a point where grounding is possible.

lost the war because of political indecision and as a result of not using military resources that were adequate to resist the British reconquest.

Today the Argentine retains this amphibious element that has such a long historical tradition, going back to the time when the country formed part of the Spanish empire, and in which are grouped some six

TRACKED VEHICLES LVTP-7

The Argentine, Brazil or Venezuela have dozens of the United States LVTP-7 amphibious tracked vehicle in its original version and also in its more modern AAV7A1. These units have been designed to transport some twenty Marine infantry from the mother ship that carries them to bridgeheads on the beach, of particular importance being the fact that they can navigate in calm waters at a speed of 13 knots when being propelled by their hydro-jets and can travel at 64 kilometers per hour on land. Its body is completely armored, incorporating a turret with armament on the upper right part, the tracks permit gradients of 60 % to be overcome and trenches up to 2,438 meters, and in its hold can be found two long benches that are reached by a large hinged rear door or from the doors at upper level. The basic model has also been modified to suit recovery and command.

thousand personnel, being famous for their deployment covering diverse sectors of the territory.

These troops report to the Commanding General of IM (CONGEIM) and are organized into diverse elements of which the 1st Brigade of IM stands out having its headquarters in the Battery Base (Base de Batteries) and includes the battalions of IM nº 1 and nº 2, an Artillery Campaign Battalion, the Commando Battalion, a Logistical Battalion, an Anti-tank Company and a Reconnaissance Company.

In the Río Gallegos base a Marine Force is established with battalions of infantry, one of Control and other logistical, whilst in the Port of Belgrano is found an Amphibious Support Force that includes a Battalion of Amphibious Vehicles, the 1st. Battalion of Field Artillery, the 1st. Battalion of Antiaircraft Artillery, the 1st. Battalion of Communications and a Company of amphibious engineers.

These forces have nearly a hundred wheeled and tracked armored vehicles distributed amongst them of type ERC-90 Lynx, LVTP-7, Mowag Grenadier, LARC-5 and Panhard VCR VTT and VDCA; the artillery includes items of M101 and M56 of 105 millimeter, M114 of 155 mm and mortars of 81 mm; the anti-tank defense is assured by non-recoiling M40A1 guns of 106 mm and Mamba and Mathogo antitank missiles; anti-aircraft defense is configured by antiaircraft guns of 30mm and missile launchers RBS-70 and Blowpipe, whilst an element of aviation consisting of a dozen apparatus UH-1H is currently being organized. Its naval deployment is effected by the support of some twenty disembarkement launches of LCM and LCVP type, and currently negotiations are underway to acquire an LST from the United States of "Newport" type in substitution of "Cabo San Antonio" that was retired several years ago.

The most prepared

The Infantry Corps of the Marine (CIM) of the Chilean Navy, that responds to the slogan "Fortis atque fidelis", consists of units deployed throughout the length of the entire country. Standing out amongst these are the Detachments of the Marine Infantry (DIM) n° 1 "Lynch" based in Iquique, the n° 2 "Miller" of Concon, the N° 3 "Sargento Aldea" in the Naval Base of Talcahuano and the n° 4 "Cochrane" in Punta Arenas, encompassing in each of the above mentioned infantry battalions and support groups of any of the specialist types that are included in the Corps; in addition there exists a fifth Unit that is the Commando Group n° 51 in Las Salinas and other smaller elements such as those afloat with the Navy, in Easter Island or in garrisons of the four naval areas.

In the above mentioned, some 5,200 men are deployed who are noted for their high degree of preparation. The officers are trained in the Naval school of "Arturo

Rifle
In Venezuela the assault rifle FAL of the Belgian company FN is used, an armament that fires munitions of 7.62 millimeters caliber and which includes versions provided with a stock folding to one side.

Prat" of Valparaíso in which they undertake two years of basic training and two of specialized study, being able to choose between the different branches of Commandos, Combat Engineering Intelligence or Telecommunications; this initial period is completed with a stay at the Marine Infantry School "Comandante Jaime Charles" in Fuerete Vergara, whilst the general troops are trained in the Center for Instruction of Recruits at Talcahuano and later follows a course of theoretical-practical training, completed with specific studies, that permit them to rise to the rank of 1st. sergeant.

To their notable preparation, which includes deployment in the mountainous regions of the country or in the arid steppes of the northern region, one must add the high level of supply of material and equipment. The personal uniform is of national production but following the lines of the "Woodland" of United States, the helmet is the M-85 "Fritz" of Kevlar, the belting is supplied by a Chilean Wienecke company and the personal arma-

ment is based on the German assault rifles Heckler und Köck (H&K) 33E and the Colt M-16, in its standard and "Commando" versions, produced in the United States.

The most outstanding support elements include the sub-rifles Famae SAF, the precision rifles H&K MGS-90, the Korean light machine guns Ultimax 100, the 40 mm grenade launchers that may be fitted to the assault rifles, the Spanish MG-42 medium machine guns, Israeli B-300 grenade launchers, etc., weapons completed with medium mortars of 81 mm artillery pieces of 105 and 155 mm, tracked vehicles with dual cabins Bv-206D, 20 mm anti-aircraft guns, portable "Blowpipe" missile systems and some thirty "Scorpion" light tanks equip-

Communications
This modern Volvo vehicle has been modified by the Argentines as a mobile communication element that integrates into its exterior the supports for the antennae and in its interior the equipment that operates on UHF, VHF and HF bands.

Marksmanship
These Venezuelan infantry of the Marine are trained in the employment of the solid and effective medium machine gun FN MAG, an armament that is very accurate when fired from a tripod that permits greater stability when firing.

ped with low pressure 76 mm guns. The amphibious movements are carried out thanks to the support of four LST ships, that include the "Valdivia" supplied by the United States and three of "Maipo" type based on the French model "Batral, and on two LSM units of "Elicura" type, using pneumatic boats powered by outboard motors to carry out transport bet-

Mobility
The Chileans have incorporated Swedish dual cabin Bv-206D vehicles that have been manufactured under license and are very useful for enabling the troops to move on any type of terrain; notable being their positive flotation that allows them to overcome areas with water.

ween ships and beach.

Specialty maintained in other countries

There are a significant number of countries that maintain marine infantry specialty units within their respective navies or inclu-

ded as a further element of its Armed Forces, it being a notable fact that some of these are very significant elements counting on dozens of thousands of men and others not counting on more than a hundred.

Those of larger implantation

Brazil is the country of South America with the largest number of Marines amongst its troops counting on some fifteen thousand men of the specialty deployed between an Amphibious Division, in which are included three Infantry battalions and one of Commando type, an Artillery Group, 1st. Command Battalion and one of Support, a Special Operations Group of independent status and eight naval security groups that cover the bases of Aratu, Belem, Ladarió, Natal, Río Grande do Sul, Río de Janeiro and So Pedro de Aldeia in each of the seven military districts and the headquarters of Brasilia.

Its most significant resources are some twenty tracked armored amphibious LVTP-7, Brazilian EE-9 CASCAVEL and EE-11 URUTU wheeled armored vehicles, modern British artillery pieces of 105 mm type "Light Gun", sophisticated anti-tank missile systems BILL of Swedish origin and portable anti-aircraft missile launchers "Igla" acquired under a curious purchase

Grenade launchers
The Mechem MGL6 is a semi-automatic weapon of South African origin that has been designed to fire cartridges of 40 millimeter that are stored in a circular drum, it is outstanding for clearing large areas in a short space of time.

from Russia. In order to carry out Amphibious assaults it counts on two LSD of "Ceara" type with an outstanding the floodable dock and platform in the stern from which helicopters SH-3D "Sea King" and AS-332F1 "Super Puma" can operate, the LST "Mattoso Maia" and diverse lesser ships of LCU, LCM and LCP type.

Another country with a high number of specialized troops is Colombia, which maintains a force of 7,500 soldiers prepared to carry out amphibious actions with the support of various models of small launches for fluvial vigilance and of eight LCU of "Morrosquillo" type. Its basic mission is the vigilance of the numerous navigable rivers that exceed 12,600 kilometers in length and that form the routes used by guerrillas and drug traffickers in their movements, at the same time constituting an element of rapid response in the case of any crisis

with other countries.

The most important forces deployed include the First Fluvial Brigade with five battalions –numbers 50, 60, 70, 80 and 90– configured with personnel trained in river knowledge and tactics, the First Atlantic Marine Infantry Brigade with headquarters in Sincelejo and including three Marine Battalions and one of soldiers specializing in anti-guerrilla warfare, and the Second Marine Infantry Brigade in Buenaventura that is made up of the rifle brigades numbers 2 and 6 and the counter-guerrilla Battalion n° 30. Their resources stand out for their lightness in order to facilitate action in the specific terrain over which these troops must move.

In Venezuela there are some five thousand infantry grouped into four tactical combat units that report to two operatio-

Lorries
In operations where a high loading capacity is required, such as for the towing of 155 millimeter artillery pieces, the Chileans use these Mercedes lorries that have been fitted with fording equipment to permit them to move in beachhead areas.

nal Commands. These are composed of four amphibious assault battalions, that are known locally as tactical combat units and are equipped with light weapons such as disposable antitank rocket launchers AT4, an armored battalion with tracked vehicles type LVTP-7 and wheeled resources such as the EE-11 URUTU or the German Fuchs, an anti-aircraft Defense Battalion with 40 mm guns, a Battalion of engineers, a Transport Battalion, an Artillery Group with M56 pieces of 105 mm and mortars of differing calibers, two units of parachute commandos and a Naval Police Regiment.

These resources are transported by means of four "Canapa" type LST displacing 4,070 tons at full load and noted for their modern construction having been built in Korea in the mid 80´s , these ships being supported by two LCU of "Margarita" type manufactured in the United States and with a displacement of nearly 400 tons.

Ecuador has three battalions formed with some 1,900 personnel, of which two are dedicated to carrying out vigilance at bases in the Galápagos Islands, Guayaquil, Jaramijó and San Lorenzo, that do not have heavy weapons and maintain an old

LST that entered service in 1945 and which may not be operative after having suffered a fire in 1998. Five British launches of LCU type are maintained as minor craft.

In Uruguay, a Battalion is maintained based on three Marine Infantry companies and one of Commando type specializing in special actions related to amphibious assault, a small force that contains some four hundred men that normally displaces with the support of half a dozen launches of type LCM6 and LCVP. For its part Paraguay has formed a Battalion of Marine Infantry and another of Commandos

CHILEAN EQUIPMENT

The Chilean Marine infantry have at their disposal a modern and varied range of personal equipment that permits them to successfully carry out their tasks. This includes helmets of Kevlar model M-85 for head protection, tactical jackets for transporting a good part of their personal equipment, rucksacks to provide mobility for such items necessary to support the rigors of the area of deployment, assault rifles Heckler und Köck 33K of 5.56x45 millimeter caliber that are noted for their retrac-

table stock and being able to locate a scope over the bolt mechanism, belting to facilitate movement in the most aggressive of areas and complements that serve to move easily in water.
They also have at their disposition other elements such as machetes, observation binoculars or crossbows with optical sights noted for their effectiveness at short range and because of their very discreet utilization.

Specialization
The LARC-5 is a United States vehicle that has been designed with hull and rear propulsion units that permit it to navigate from a mother ship to the coast, its function being associated with logistical tasks of transport.

with some 50,000 trained soldiers that do not have the support of specific ships but normally work together with transport helicopters UH-1H.

Peru deploys some 3,000 infantry within an Amphibious Brigade, with two active battalions and one Reconnaissance Company and a Group of Commandos-Divers that operate in an independent manner. An outstanding feature of the Brigade is a Company of Armored vehicles that includes wheeled armor of type V-100 and V-200 "Chaimite", light and heavy mortars, recoilless guns, light anti-aircraft pieces and some BMR-600 of Spanish origin, vehicles outstanding for their agility, armoring and incorporate modifications that permit them to navigate from transport ships to the coast.

The Dominican Republic maintains only a small unit of naval infantry.

The situation in Central America
This area includes countries such as Costa Rica, Guatemala, Nicaragua and Panama that do not have forces specifically trained for amphibious assault within their military organizations. In spite of this, in this area is found Mexico that enjoys large

strength in the specialty deploying some 8,000 men divided between the 1st. and the 4th. brigades, units that have their Headquarters in Vera Cruz and Manzanillo respectively; their equipment being modern but light, including the Pegaso VAP lorries that have been designed with a body that permits the vehicle to navigate and move on land without any problem of continuity.

Likewise two battalions of independent Artillery have been formed that have been assigned Italian M56 pieces of 105 mm, recoilless guns of 106 mm of M40A1 model and medium mortars of 81 mm, units that are located at Frontera and Puerto Madero. Also worth mentioning

is the Battalion deployed to ensure the security of the President of the Republic, the Para-Commando Regiment that is trained for all types of special actions and the naval force consisting of three United States LST dating from the period of the Second World War and an LSD of "Thomaston" type that is maintained in reserve since having been presented by the U.S. Navy.

El Salvador deploys 150 naval infantry and maintains launches of type LCM used principally for the transport of light material, whilst Honduras has formed a battalion of Marines that can be supported by a modern ship of LCU type acquired from Florida in 1988 and named "Punta Caxinas". The FNH 1491, as it has been designated, has a displacement of 625 tons, at full load, has a maximum speed of 14 knots and can transport 100,000 kilograms of all types of material.

Armor
The BMR-600 are wheeled armored units, with 6x6 traction, manufactured in Spain and acquired by the Peruvians for their Marine Infantry troops, circumstance that obliges modification with fording equipment.

Transport

In order to organize an amphibious assault operation with guarantees of success previous planning to study defenses of the enemy must be carried out together with the deployment of adequate ships to permit the disembarkment of a superior force.

A large number of the most important countries of the world, and particularly those that have naval fleets and large coastlines to guard, have created infantry units specializing in carrying out amphibious assault as an element of particular strength in dissuading hostile actions by third parties.

These units correspond to two basic types ; the first includes those that have been formed, whether individually or in combination with various countries, and must be activated to carry out a specific action, for which reason they remain on standby –"on call"– being the applied terminology until such time as their

Movements

Some countries still have transport units in service that do not have floodable docks and recur to the use of on board cranes to disembark transported vehicles and equipment to the launches - a slower operation that involves greater risk.

deployment is decided, requiring several days to prepare and initiate their transfer up to the point of action. The second is that which the United States maintains and that combines forces such as the above with others, the MEU (Marine Expeditionary Unit), that is always found navigating in various seas and oceans of the planet, its arrival at the working area being faster, particularly taking into account the diverse points of the globe where pre-positioned warehouses are located and in which large quantities of

vehicles, armament systems and logistical elements are kept.

Amphibious operations

These are military operations in which the naval power is targeted over a point on the coast in order to place on the beach or on land a force that has been transported to the area benefitting from the specific characteristics of the amphibious transport ships - supported at times by civilian ships hired to this effect-, ships that permit movement wherever their intervention is

Transport of helicopters
Successive waves of helicopters, such as these six British Westland "Commando", permit the placing of the amphibious troops transported to the predetermined location. As a result of their capacity, more than one hundred men together with their personal equipment and support weapons may be carried in each group rotation.

required and conferring a large strategic capacity limited only by the need for refueling and food supply, this being transported in logistical support ships that accompany them in their transfer.

Four basic types

Basically, the amphibious operations may be grouped into the following categories or methods of action: The Amphibious Assault, the Amphibious Retreat, the Amphibious Demonstration and the Amphibious Incursion. These are differentiated between each other according to the final objective that is desired as a result of the same; the quantity of resources required to carry out each of them and the movements associated to complete them.

The first is the largest and has the objective of arriving on the coast in order to proceed to physical occupation of the objectives on land that have previously been established, for which it requires

transport ships that are assigned to carry out movements as far as the target area, elements of transport that can deploy resources from the above to the targeted beach and a Disembarkation Force of sufficient size to guarantee the success of the mission. Once on the coast they will proceed to establish a bridgehead that may spread over one or various neighboring beaches in order to then move both inland and around the flanks in order to establish a foothold, with a depth and extension pre-

viously established at the beginning of the attack necessary to destroy the defenses established by the enemy and prevent them from obtaining potential reinforcements

Support
This launch is loaded with heavy engineering machinery that will be deployed in the spearhead of the amphibious assault to support the movement of launches and vehicles during their deployment grounding on the beach.

"Small fish"
The launches leave the floodable dock one by one and travel to a position where they start navigating in circles waiting for the order to advance quickly to the coast. This navigation is called "small fish".

via elements arriving from other locations.

This physical establishment of a large element of combat usually requires a great effort in logistical support and resources in the first phase of the action, aiming to push the enemy inland. Its execution usually lasts several days until such time as the final points of deployment can be achieved and requires an important quantity of resources to achieve it, with a solid political support to underwrite the cost in resources and lives that are usually associated with its carrying out in areas where it is assumed there will be a reaction from the enemy, this being the case in the amphibious assaults undertaken by the British in the Straits of San Carlos during the Falklands war, movements that provided the power to locate a military Force on land that finally obtained control of that southern territory that had been invaded by Argentine troops.

Operations of assault

For its part the Amphibious Retreat is the opposite operation to the above. It is carried out in order to reach a hostile or potentially hostile coast, with a naval group that has the principal mission of

Troops
The LCM-6 type launch can carry fifty men who gain access to them by hanging from nets located to starboard and port, as in this case, or from the floodable docks.

helping to re-embark one of its own forces that is deployed there. It requires local air support and surface combat resources, normally submarines and frigates, that cover its own transport activities and avoid the reaction of the enemy, given that the troops that arrive at the beach and land in launches are very vulnerable to attack from the enemy, who will endeavor to neutralize the action.

If the action is carried out at a point and in a tactical situation where no reaction of the enemy occurs only a landing process is involved that requires nothing more complex than the correct planning of coastal movements of ships to transfer men and resources to the latter and that

will occupy holds, cabins and platforms assigned for transit to its own base or to a new location where a possible assault may be planned.

The Amphibious Demonstration is a simulation that has the objective of making the enemy believe that an Amphibious Assault is about to take place in a one or more locations. The simple demonstration of a force, whether real or fictitious, will cause the movement of troops and resources of the country subject to the incursion in order to defend its coasts and against the possibility of the same, assault that finally may not take place or will occur in a very different location to that implied by the Demonstration.

During the Gulf War of 1991, an operation of this type took place off the coast of Kuwait. The Iraqis, who had occupied the neighboring country, deployed various mechanized divisions and combat tanks to the coast with the object of delaying the landing of United States Marines, an action that the press had been entrusted to publish in order to mislead the Iraqi infor-

mation services. What really happened was that small groups of SEALs and Marine commandos, landed and provoked large explosions on certain beaches making the enemy believe that full scale landing was taking place. What had really happened was that these same Marines had formed a force that advanced at that very moment by land as a further element in the allied progression that would lead to the defeat of the subjects of the president of Iraq.

An Amphibious Incursion is of minor scale than the first of the above and has, as its objective, the rapid conquering of an objective on land or the temporary occupation of a land area. Since the aim is to obtain local superiority through the use of reduced resources and in a short time, its carrying out is based on a rapid action , potent and precise that, usually, is undertaken utilizing resources of small size that can be deployed quickly and withdrawn quickly thanks to the use of aerial means and terrestrial transports such as hovercrafts.

Methods of transport

Amphibious operations are very complex military actions insofar as their planning and execution are concerned, for which reason they require very varied resources to carry them out: surface ships for the transport of the disembarking force, escort ships and submarines to protect the movement of these and the discharging at the coast, the necessary naval support fire, aerial resources that are assigned the task of first obtaining local superiority and then carrying out transport between ships and the beach, and lastly the disembarking force that must include men and equipment adequate to carry out the mission.

AIR CUSHION VEHICLES LCAC

The "Landing Craft Air Cushion" correspond to a series of ninety one air-cushioned vehicles designed to provide mobility to large of the United States Marine Corps and to place elements on the beach elements ranging from logistical elements to combat tanks. Their design, with two large turbines in the stern and a retractable ramp in the bow permit them to operate in some 70 % of the coastal regions of the world, percentage that is far superior to the 15 % applicable to launches.
Four Avco-Lycoming FT-40B gas turbines propel these units at a maximum speed of 40 knots when loaded, having a range at this speed of around 200 miles. Its armament is configured by two heavy M-2 of 12.70 machine guns as weapons for self defense, includes on a principal deck for navigation that integrates surface radar and is capable of transporting loads of up to 75 tons; the air cushions that are inflated in the lower part to facilitate displacement over the surface of the water and permit movements on land.

Speed
The employment of pneumatic assault vessels, propelled by potent outboard motors, permit the carrying of contingents of soldiers who will establish the first positions and support the arrival of following assault waves.

Specialized ships

Traditionally an evolution of models has taken place that has followed the naming and types established by the United States according to the type of mission to be carried out, the tendency in recent years being to construct ships of greater multi-utilization and with a capacity to release the elements transported by sea and air and which, if necessary, can be used as support in situations such as civil catastrophe, humanitarian aid operations or transport of intervention forces, criteria

Grounding
The disembarking launches arrive at the beach and open their doors in the bow, or in some cases also in the stern, so that the transported elements may, under their own volition, reach the shoreline and progress inland.

which has motivated an increase in the medical resources embarked and the logistical areas designated for food, spare parts and replacements.

The classification of the most important naval units includes the LHA (Landing Helicopter Attack) that has a displacement of around 30,000 tons and that is outstanding for its large flight-deck, from which a notable quantity of helicopters and vertical take-off aircraft may operate, and

integrating a large capacity for loads released to the exterior via a dock that can be flooded in the prow permitting the exit of launches and amphibious assault vehicles. This last detail also applies to the LHD (Landing Helicopter Dock) that has similar dimensions but that is orientated to activities particularly related to transport and is provided with multiple use properties.

For their part the LPH (Landing Platform Helicopter) follow a concept that is

Material

In order to support a Force operating in enemy territory it is necessary to count on sufficient resources and vehicles. For this, the amphibious assault ships accompany the LSTs that have the mission of transporting large quantities of transport and combat vehicles.

older but has developed to give rise to ships, such as the British "Ocean", with large potential and with outstanding capacities, the ship to shore movements passing to a substantial employment of transport helicopters that are carried aboard and which are transported either on the principal deck or in an interior hold that is accessed via large lifts.

Smaller, but of a more multi-purpose type, for which reason they are widely used by nations with navies of medium size, are the LPD (Landing Platform Dock), vessels that combine projection of elements from the stern deck where small groups of helicopters can operate or from the dock that can be flooded in which landing launches may be loaded. The

Assault

The troops move with quickly and with agility during the first moment of arrival at the beach because at this location they are very vulnerable to enemy fire. Later they will consolidate an area, establishing defensive and logistical positions, and will initiate their advance to a predetermined position.

LSD (Landing Ship Dock) are more orientated vehicle support missions, loads, and troops, although the capacity to offload that which is transported has not been forgotten.

Specifically for the transport of combat tanks and mechanical means are the LST (Landing Ship Tank) that usually have elements in the bow so that this type of vehi-

cle can directly reach dock or beach, being able to unite to this zone via groups of floating pontoons. Their loading capacity makes them suitable for use by smaller nations to move contingents of troops and vehicles between islands or as elements of low level dissuasion.

Rapid assault

In front of the above mentioned ships are to be found the landing launches that are usually transported in their interior and serve to place all that which has been carried up to the point of attack on the beach. Those of larger size are denominated LCT (Landing Craft Tank), and they may operate in an independent manner in order to overcome distances greater than 1,000 miles and are noted for their loading capacity that permits them to carry all types of vehicles and material.

The LCU (Landing Craft Utility) are

Assault
The first waves of amphibious movement include the deployment of very rapid vessels such as these Dutch launches of solid construction propelled by outboard motors that enable the transport of the initial nucleus having the task of taking possession of the bridgehead.

somewhat smaller than the above, for which reason their loading capacity is lesser, and they are used to transfer mechanical vehicles and auto-propelled batteries to the beach. The LCM (Landing Craft Medium) type is subdivided into variants 8 and 6, the former being larger and more multi-use and the latter of lesser displacement and adapted to the transport of men; to the above must be added the LCVP (Landing Craft Vehicles Personnel) for light vehicles and soldiers, the LCP/LCPL (Landing Craft Personnel) being only for

Dutch
The L9536 corresponds to a modern class of amphibious assault vessel placed into service in Holland to provide mobility to its troops. A design feature is the covered transport zone to protect men from adverse meteorological conditions.

these last mentioned and of rigid and semi-rigid hulls.

Likewise, diverse models of air cus-

hioned vehicles have been developed –hovercrafts– that permit very rapid movement of troops and personnel, with the ability to arrive at locations situated several hundred meters from the coast and thus overcome the first line of defense. Because of their cost and complexity, these vessels are used by few countries, amongst which Russia and the United States stand out, including amongst the models used by the first of these the enormous "Pomornik" propelled by three large turbo propellers at the stern, enabling a speed of 60 knots to be achieved and in its interior three combat tanks or three hundred totally equipped men can be carried, and the even faster "Dzhey-

ran" that can reach 70 knots and has its own anti-aircraft defense based on guns and missile launchers.

For their part the United States makes extensive use of its LSAC (Landing Craft Air-Cushion) that are used for moving combat tanks and wheeled armored vehicles up to the coast, some of which were used to re-conquer a Kuwaiti island that had been occupied by Iraqis in 1990.

Good handling and rapid movement are possessed by the diverse medium and heavy transport helicopters associated with the ship to coastal movements, being also very adequate for combining with attack helicopters that they will accompany in order to provide escort or serving to attack

terrestrial or mobile enemy positions. These vehicles will be assigned to carry men in the first phase and later carry loads, either in the interior of the cabin or suspended from slings, in the later stages of logistical support and of the arrival of complementary resources.

Carrying out the assault

As with all military operations, those of amphibious type require specific planning that will be initiated by a political decision to prepare a force of this type in order to resolve a particular incident, establishing the initial assumptions that will mark their action and defining what will be the principal objectives in the carrying out

DISEMBARKING LAUNCHES LCM-8

This type of launch is used in many countries in order to provide mobility to vehicles, mechanical means, artillery elements or soldiers, serving also for the transport of logistical resources such as munitions, fuel or food. Its size and equipment is ideal for operating from the floodable docks of diverse types of assault ships in which 2 or 4 of these launches fit in order to quickly deploy their potential to the coast.

In the case of Spain, to which Navy the launch illustrated with this commentary belongs, these are units constructed

in shipyards in California and in the factory of San Fernando of the State Company Bazán. These are models that displace between 115 and 120 tons at full load and whose outstanding feature are the dimensions of 22.7 meters length, 6.6 width and 1.8 draught. It is propelled by four diesel motors GM 6-71 that provide a total of 696 horsepower turning two propellers in the stern, obtaining speeds of up to 11 knots, its crew is made up of five men and its construction in steel plate permits easy repair after suffering blows or breakage resulting from its special duties.

Deployment

Modern amphibious assault units, such as the Dutch L800 "Rotterdam", can transport four launches of type LCM-8 in its interior and various helicopters on the poop deck, resources with which the ship to coast movements may be organized.

of the same.

In order for an action of this type to be chosen it is essential that flexibility, of which it is a characteristic, is fundamental in function of the objectives to be achieved, the mobility derived from the landing in transport ships permitting use at the most convenient moment, and the element of surprise as a result of lack of knowledge of where and when action will take place –usually at the weakest point of defense of the enemy– landing will take place, requiring for its correct execution very specialized personnel, following very special procedures and training and deriving from a particular type of organization.

Phases of the operation.

The first action to be carried out is that of planning that will commence with the arrival of a command order that will define the mission to be undertaken, the Force that must carry it out and other significant instructions. The members of the high command of the landing force and of the Naval Force will initiate their activities by taking, in a coordinated manner, a series of decisions with relation to requirements and

necessities.

The following phase is the landing of all material, men and equipment onto the ships that will transport them, a process that usually takes place in ports and naval bases and counts on the assistance of cranes and elements established there. The entrance onto the ships is made in accordance with a specific plan in function of the later disembarking, in order that elements do not interfere with each other.

With the above finalized, the transit to the area where the objective is located commences, navigation that will be made under the escort of other types of ship that avoid any threat from the air, surface or under water. This transfer will be accom-

panied by an exercise, at some point along the way, in order to determine possible defects and correct incidents deriving therefrom.

Finally the assault will be carried out and this will be initiated by deploying combat divers who prepare accurate cartographic maps and clear obstacles and mines in the area, and members of special units that carry out reconnaissance missions in depth or the destruction of systems of vigilance. In a coordinated manner and at hour H –usually at night– the movement of launches and helicopters towards the beach will commence, using naval and aircraft fire to destroy positions defending the area.

This is the most critical of the phases because it entails the highest degree of risk and requires a high level of coordination, superiority being fundamental in order to take the beach and initiate a progression without restrictions.

Port

There some types of amphibious assault in which initial engagements with hostile forces are not envisaged, as is the case when providing humanitarian assistance or interposition, for that reason disembarking will be carried out directly to the quays of ports.

Landing

The launches permit the transport of infantry up to the proximity of the coastline. Once there they open their doors and carry out a rapid landing so that the first units may progress up to positions inland, moments in which they are highly exposed to enemy fire.

From the moment at which the amphibious assault is launched, hovercrafts or other types of vessels initiate their navigation, both rapid and discrete in order to avoid detection that would give sufficient time for them to be neutralized, the carrying out of movements will have been perfectly planned, from the time that the first man sets foot on land, through to the support that will be needed to maintain the force that has been disembarked at the location and over the duration envisaged for the action.

Progressive arrival

The first to arrive on the beach must be the infantry that constitutes the primary combat element facing the enemy positions established in the area, a nucleus of defense that will have been attacked days previously by commando groups infiltrated by air and sea in order to survey terrain and that will also have been hammered by artillery fire from the 76, 115 and 127 millimeter guns of the escort ships and these enemy positions will also have been the target for guided bombs, rockets and gun fire from fighter bombers –usually Harrier

Assault

Whilst the men advance towards the interior in order to consolidate their positions, the launches continue to arrive with more vehicles that will serve to support the action, those that are seen in this shot being a self-propelled howitzer of 155 mm together with its magazine.

vertical take-off aircraft- and support and attack helicopters that will accompany them.

Taking position

Launches of type LCM-6 and LCM-8 or air cushioned vehicles will displace under cover of the night in order to make their localization and destruction difficult –the action is usually initiated at about three in the morning so that the first units may land about an hour later at the beach– and will arrive full of troops, soldiers who will themselves wade the few meters that separate them from the beach, and once there, will remove the life jackets designed to aid flotation in the water taking into account the heavy equipment being carried.

They will establish positions with light and medium machine guns, deploying light antitank systems of disposable rocket-launcher type and wire guided equipment to face mechanical means together with positions with armament systems, placing a protective anti-aircraft umbrella based on light launchers of diverse of short range infra-red missiles systems. In parallel, transport helicopters will place other groups of infantry to more advanced positions, in which emplacements will be set up to avoid any enemy counter-attack that may occur, in order to assist the resources deployed on the beach.

On one of the flanks an assault group has been located with armored amphibious tracked vehicles, with a capacity for some twenty men, notable for their ability to

navigate in water thanks to hydro-jets that propel them and having a body sufficiently resistant to ward off impact from light arms and flack. These tracked vehicles will progress some three hundred meters towards the interior and will have opened the doors in the rear so that troops may disembark and take position before initiating the advance in coordination with the other elements deployed in the area.

Supporting the action

Together with the resources arriving beforehand a specialized group will have been deployed to support the movement of vessels, their function being to signal the points of contact for the above mentioned and marking positions by means of lanterns and chemical lights so as to assist

TRACKED VEHICLE FV4018

In order to support the movement of vessels at the beach and assist them to escape from possible grounding the BARV (Beach Armored Recovery Vehicle) that is used by the British Royal Marines has been designed for use during amphibious assaults on all kinds of beaches. This machine has been designed on the basis of the Centurion combat tank of Leyland Motors that was placed into production at the end of the 40's. Based on the above, which confers a notable mobility in loosely compacted sand of the beach and including within the

water if the depth so permits, a superstructure has been installed to replace the turret and gun. Its large dimensions permit the vehicle to operate in areas with a water depth of 2,895 meters, and incorporates a hatch in the top from which the Commander of the machine directs the movements. Its crew is composed of four men, it weighs 40,643 kilograms and twelve machines of this particular model have been constructed, of which three are deployed with British amphibious ships.

Support
The landing actions require a strong concentration of fire in a reduced space. For this reason the landed troops are deployed with weapons such as this light mortar with which they cover the arrival of their colleagues.

launches that may encounter problems in their beaching. This assistance will be placed with the help of bulldozers and the employment of cable winches that serve to raise the door of launches that have been damaged or suffered impact.

Also deployed in the area will be an element given the task of organizing and managing the repeated arrival of equipment and material, a coordination that requires management of powerful communication systems and the planning of

Transmissions
This French wheeled armored vehicle is configured as a mobile center for transmissions that permit contact between the landed elements, the Command aboard the ships and the Command Headquarters located hundreds or thousands of kilometers away.

supply chains needed to maintain these in accordance with necessity.

This initial infantry chain and light support armament will be reinforced with the arrival of more LCM-8 launches and hovercraft in which will be transported all-terrain vehicles carrying weapons such as TOW long range missile launchers, wheeled armored vehicles to support the advance movements and mobile Command centers permitting the establishment of points of coordination serving as a bridge between units on the coast and Command Headquarters aboard the transport vessels.

New waves
Several hours have now passed since

BEACH-HEAD MOVEMENTS

Combats

In order to dislodge the adversary from defensive positions a large force of weapons must be deployed from the ships and the beach. In these actions medium mortars of 81 mm firing grenades with a range in excess of ive kilometers are particularly useful.

the amphibious assault commenced and various rotations of transport have taken place over the designated area, neutralizing the small pockets of enemy resistance that were found deployed there.

The superiority in the air obtained prior to starting the action, naval superiority arising from the contingent of surface vessels and submarines deployed in the area to support and protect the amphibious assault vessels, and terrestrial superiority in the coastal area obtained as a result of the initial combats, permit the continuance of the plan established in the previous stage of the assault.

Elements of consolidation

It is now time to initiate the deploy-

Resources

Launches and self propelled pontoons such as this in the photograph continue to transport heavy vehicles that, as with combat tanks, use their fire to support the actions of the troops on land in their progressive movement inland.

ment of mechanical and armored resources that will permit the making up of formations capable of penetrating dozens of kilometers towards the interior in order to secure an area of large enough dimensions to serve as a base for launching later operations.

Towed howitzers arrive in slings hanging from some of the heavy transport helicopters and also boxes of ammunition and even pneumatic containers loaded with fuel, elements that may be placed accurately by the aircraft prior to returning quickly to ship in order to continue with new transports. At sea, the capacity of the LCM-8 launches is used to provide mobility to the heavier systems, such as

auto-propelled howitzers and their munitions or medium combat tanks, vehicles that require particular care during their exit from the launches to avoid their becoming stuck in the sandy floor of the beach.

As a third phase, and now during daylight, auto-propelled floating pontoons will be constructed that will be transported attached to the hull of the LST type ships. These large dimension pontoons may be united between each other and located at the bow of this type of ship so that vehicles of all types transported in their interior may pass from the holds, via the ramp, onto the dock situated in the water, an element that can then be

Irresistible
Medium machine guns, such as these British L7, fire belted munitions at rates of some 700 rounds per minute, a rate that serves to provide an irresistible and precise support fire covering the areas to be overcome.

transported to the coast thanks to groups of engines serving as propulsion units.

These pontoons can arrive on the beach and serve to land, in a single operation, enormous quantities of vehicles with loads that supply necessary needs, returning once more to the ships to be reloaded. Depending on the type of vessels employed for the action, the potential of their enormous cranes may be employed to discharge heavy elements located in holds and place them directly on to pontoons or launches.

Conclusion of the assault
Following the deployment of the combat elements the placement of logistical units must be initiated, in order to support the movements of these, for which reason mobile repair units are deployed, along with bases for the evacuation of the injured, deposits with fuel to form locations for refueling, logistical equipment to facilitate the maintenance of the deployed Force and all equipment necessary to ease the planned task.

This prodigious force of men, resources and equipment, deployed at times over various adjoining beaches to constitute a wider front to reduce the capacity of the enemy to react, will take place over only two or three days –time necessary to consolidate an area chosen to this effect– in which a strong reaction from the enemy is not expected. The positions established in depth by the mechanized columns, that will have advanced without having contact with entities of the same magnitude, will permit the consolidation of the first phase in order to initiate later ones. These will be the arrival of new contingents of troops and terrestrial resources that will not necessarily be Marine infantry and who will expand the size of the advance up to domination of the physical space necessary to exploit the potential for action, or the deployment of elements capable of providing a great variety of support services, in the case of the operation being allied to supposed humanitarian aid and being positioned between two opposing forces.

The consolidation of operations, the advance inland, the assurance that that the area remains free of hostile elements and other small enclaves will be the point of inflexion permitting re-emplacement of elements of the Marine infantry who were the first to be landed and exposed to singular effort associated with initial attrition. The Marines may return to their ships together with their most characteristic resources so as to commence a transfer that will return them to their bases or, after a period of rest and recuperation, to another point where their deployment is necessary , honoring their slogan of "undertaking terrestrial operations initiated at sea".

Hovercrafts
The advantage of these means of assault is that they can transport notable quantities of wheeled and tracked vehicles to more secure advanced positions where they may be landed quickly to avoid their neutralization.

THE TRAINING OF THE UNITED STATES MARINES

School

The "Basic School" of Quantico in Virginia is the principal training center of the Command of the United States Marine Corps, men and women who will lead their combat units in the most varied of tactical situations.

"Making Marines, winning battles" is one of the slogans of the United States Marine Corps (USMC) defining in a clear and concise form the spirit of the Corps in the training of its one hundred and seventy thousand personnel.

The success obtained by this type of troops up to the present –in the decade of the 90's they have intervened in a hundred conflicts–, participating in the most varied of scenarios and applying the most modern combined resource techniques to obtain domination in terrestrial combat, is based on the meticulous, rigorous and strict process of selection and training of its components, giving priority to the human element before the rest of the elements which form this organization.

The projection of that expected for the immediate future passes through an application of a new process of personal preparation which will be applied to a new concept of collective employment which will substantially increase the capacity of these elements of specialized men in amphibious war with overhead coverage.

Changing process

The publication of documents such as the "Operational Maneuver from the Sea" (OMFTS) of 1996 which describes a new approach to the projection of naval power, the "Joint Vision 2010" which sets out the prevision of the Joint Chiefs of Staff for the second decade of the 21st century, or

Theory

In Camp Lejeune the Marines are prepared in those activities necessary for later use in their tasks with guarantees of success, training which includes theory classes in open air installations.

THE TRAINING OF THE UNITED STATES MARINES

the "Sea Dragon" which establishes the use of current technological resources to obtain a change in philosophy in operational concepts, are some of the paths being followed to undertake a profound process of change which will make the Marines more lethal and effective and permit the carrying out of more varied activities requiring greater technical knowledge.

Laboratory for evaluation

In Quantico, in the state of Virginia a "Commandant's Warfighting Laboratory" (CWL) has been established since the end of 1995, which serves as an element of trial and validation of new operational concepts, improvement in tactics, more advanced techniques and updated procedures, changes which are being introduced in a progressive manner and coinciding with new systems, in the USMC.

Between the years 1996 and 2000 an experimental plan of five years was applied. This is directed by the CWL and implies the application of an open development project designated "Sea Dragon", a process which is divided into three phases: the first known as "Hunter Warrior" now completed, the second "Urban Warrior" from which the last conclusions

Teamwork
Working as a team is fundamental during the process of formation and this will also be so in the final posting. Because of this, during the training in Quantico the men will be motivated to form groups which are capable of resolving such incidents as may be put before them.

are being extracted and the third "Capable Warrior" which is being carried out at present, and which will, possibly, require an increase in the experimentation time.

Its application is carried out via the establishment of an experimental organization designated "Special Purpose Marine Air-Ground Task Force" (SPA-MAGTF(X)), which serves to evaluate the new concepts applied and which are the fruit of the conclusions extracted from the above mentioned programs, results which are applied limited objective experiments as well as advanced military projection experiments.

The problem of recruitment

The peculiar situation current in the United States, with a rate of unemployment quoted at about 5 %, and with each

Drill Instructor
This is the name given to the sergeants who are given the task of the basic training of the troops and to supervise them during the period of initial training.
This shot taken in the barracks of San Diego, corresponds to the moment when the student is corrected with regard to the position of the rifle.

THE TRAINING OF THE UNITED STATES MARINES

Hardness

The process of formation of the Marines, whether of troops or of Command, is both long and hard. With this it is expected that the result will be men trained to war, prepared and combative, from whom great potential will be obtained before all types of actions.

day that passes greater numbers of youngsters follow higher level and university studies, is giving rise to a truly competitive competition between the four constituent elements of the Armed Forces –Army, Navy, Air Force and the Marines– to recruit youngsters, both men and women, necessary to maintain their actual structures.

Attack

The Officers who attend the courses of the "Basic School" receive apprenticeship in diverse areas, one of these being that of attack with tanks and armored vehicles with resources which are to hand. In the photograph a Marine –to the left– has just thrown a Molotov cocktail at an old combat tank.

For this reason the USMC has established a program of recruitment targeted at 17 to 21 year old youngsters that form the ideal segment for conformance to the structure of troops in the units. These programs are accompanied by the maintenance of very solid recruiting teams, and this is also reinforced with improvements in living standards.

The technological transition towards the immediate future requires better qualified personnel for which reason a standard must be applied at the moment of selection, requiring mental, moral and physical

adaptation in those civilians who wish to be Marines and who will be capable of winning future battles and, at the same time, be better Americans. The preparation consists of four phases: Recruiting, Training, Cohesion and Maintenance.

The recruitment is assigned to specialist personnel who seek men and women of high quality who exceed the solicited standard, with the application of a program DEP (Delayed Entry Program) to compensate the personal defects of those who may not have achieved such minimum standard. After selection they pass through the first stage of training in which the "Drill Instructor" has great influence and who is given the task of managing the process formation of twelve weeks and which has been redefined in content and duration in order to produce a higher quality of Marine.

Basic training

This period consolidates the basic training BWT (Basic Warrior Training) together with complementary MCT (Marine Combat Training) which is provided at infantry schools, finalizing with an exercise denominated "Crucible" which consists of 54 hours of deployment in the training camp without rest, serving to reinforce aspects such as honor, courage, decision

making, reaction to problems and adversity, and team work.

In order to promote cohesion between these soldiers they pass through the School of Infantry in which they are assigned to teams following a program designated "Team Integrity". The intention is to form teams who will commence working in a joint manner and will stay together until they comply with their first posting to battalions, during the period of their initial enlistment.

In this manner an improved Maintenance in the manner of working in teams is programmed together with better mutual synchronization derived from the long period of time spent together. Thus, they will be able to obtain a higher level of output and improved conduct, which is reflected in the stated values of the Corps: "Honor, Courage, and Commitment".

Training centers

The General Command of the MCCDC (Marine Corps Combat Development Command Organization) manages the training mission which implies development of concepts, plans and doc-

Marksmanship

In order to obtain the maximum potential from training, each Marine is instructed in marksmanship with his personal weapon up to distances of 300 meters. The quality of marksmanship is looked with great care and is maintained by continued practice.

Classes

The process of formation of the future officers of the USMC includes both theoretical and practical classes, standing out amongst these last that which are carried out in the installations adjoining the "Communications Officers School" in order to understand the various computer systems associated with communications.

trine: the development of the policy and programs for the training and education of the Marine units, whether regular or reserve, and to identify the need for change in training derived from changes in the grouping of MAGTF tasks. Various areas depend on this amongst which are those dedicated to training and education and which have, at their head, the Commander of Schools of the Marine Corps.

Mission: training

Under the direct supervision of the above, and having as their principal mission the implementation of policy, plans and programs in its respective area, several education centers are found: "Non Commissioned School", Staff Non Commissioned School", "Marine Corps University", "Officer Candidates School", "The Basic School" of Camp Barrett in Quantico, "Communication Officers School", "Amphibious Warfare School" "Computer Science School", "Marine Corps Institute" in Washington and the "Command and Staff College".

These centers together with others,

have as their principal task the formation of the cadres of Command which direct the rest of the Marines in their daily activities, or those deriving from their participation in missions of combat or intervention, to which must be added the expected requirements for humanitarian aid which has been gaining a special relevance over recent years and which requires the dispatch of military elements which, as with the Marines, need a large logistical capacity with associated transport resources which have no parallel in the rest of the components of the Armed Forces of the United States.

For this reason the activities taught in these schools correspond to particular courses having a variable duration lasting from a few weeks to a complete academic course, classes which include theoretical doctrine, naval justice, planning, etc., and which also give rise to field training following a program adequate to each of the courses being taught. The personnel of the USMC, together with students from other countries invited to participate in the same, complete their personnel training with these courses and which support, in a positive manner, their training towards development of the most varied of actions in amphibious war.

Operation bases

In the process of formation, the operation bases of Camp Lejeune and Camp Pendleton are highly important, including in the first of these the base for expeditionary training, this being the most complete in the world. Thus in Lejeune is the "School of Infantry" of Camp Geiger in which 22,500 Marines and Sailors are trained each year and who pass through here to complete their "Basic Infantry Skills" of 28 days, a later stage to that of basic training at Parri's Island and prior to specialist military occupational training (MOS) defining the activity to be undertaken by each.

Initial training is also carried out at the Infantry School which qualifies specific personnel to undertake activities such as being members of infantry, machine gun operators, members of mortar teams and operators of anti-tank missiles, being the "Advanced Infantry Training Section" which undertakes the preparation of sergeants who will act as chiefs of patrols and leaders of squadrons.

At this location is found, for example, the Firing Range of "Stone Bay" which consists of 11 ranges for use of all types of weapons –from pistols to machine guns– and for distances up to 1,000 yards, being used each year by some 100,000 students who

MARINE ENHANCEMENT PROGRAM

The letters MEP identify a program which seeks to prepare a Marine who will be more lethal, based on his or her personal training and the deployment of new armaments and personal equipment.

Lighter clothes, jackets and more comfortable belting, improved and more easy to use elements of personal protection, equipment to assist in navigation in movements and a large list of elements will be used to improve the combat capacity of the Marine. This aspect also includes the introduction of various elements associated with modern weapons, such as laser equipment or opto-electronic vision systems to improve aiming, which make them more lethal. Their introduction started to be planned in September of 1994 and it was decided to apply a criteria for the acquiring of such elements to those available on the commercial market, thus reducing the cost of specific development which, over time, proved to not always give the best results. The gradual introduction of these elements is being carried out in such a way that it is coordinated with the improvements in personnel preparation, the objective of the UMSC being to maintain the same capacity during the 21st century that it has demonstrated to date.

Tactical themes

The capacity of the United States Marine Corps is based on the individual, for which reason the process of formation is fundamental and implies lectures as well as classes in the field which serve as an initial practice to prepare them their active service.

Marine units and the "Marine Corps Service Support Schools" which includes nine centers through which pass some 10,000 students each year to receive training in areas such as survival at sea or fiscal subjects.

In support of the above teaching specific installations are also available such as the "Weapons Training Battalion" at Quantico having various firing ranges for the employment of complementary arms and other areas destined for sports competitions, and it is also responsible for the maintenance of arms such as the M40A1 rifle.

carry out all their practice there and in which they use up some 20 million cartridges. In Camp Lejeune is also the "Marine Corps Engineer School" covering all the specialties of the engineers, the "Field Medical Service School" in which the medical teams prepare to work with the

Continuity

The process of separation of the Marines commences when they enter into the corps and does not finish until they retire or when they pass to the Reserve, and use is made of any time available, such as this transit via an amphibious ship, to continue with the most varied of task.

NATO: GREECE, TURKEY AND PORTUGAL

The member countries of The North Atlantic Treaty Organization provide resources to that defensive structure according to their own economies, the geo-strategic situation that they occupy and traditional differences between elements making up their Armed Forces.

In the case of amphibious forces, some nations stand out in giving greater emphasis to this type of troops because of their having notably long coastlines, as a result of having zones within their areas of influence where it is possible that they may have to deploy, or as a result of actions in times past.

Between those countries that compose part of the defensive agreement, Greece, Turkey and Portugal are of importance, providing part of their amphibious resources for the support of CAFMED (Combined Amphibious Force, Mediterranean) demonstrating a decision play a major role in the joint exercises of amphibious assault that are carried out in the Mediterranean coast and in particular

Equipment

The Greek Marine infantry is an amphibious Force that is noted for its modern equipment and for the maintenance of a solid capacity for deployment, although some elements of its equipment are out of date and need replacement.

Equipment

The Portuguese "Fuzileiros" are a Force of about two thousand five hundred men trained to carry out actions of Amphibious Assault, including a small element assigned to the joint amphibious Brigade together with Holland and Great Britain.

those of the south of Italy where much of the training is carried out.

Infantry of the Greek navy

The unusual strategic location of Greece, its continuous clashes with Turkey, the numerous islands of the Aegean sea that form part of its territory and other imposed conditions have given rise to the formation of a specialized force that depends on the Army of that country, but operates in a continuous manner with the assault ships of the Navy.

These men, grouped into a Unit typical of a Brigade, is a Force consisting of some three thousand men with barracks in the Base of Voules on the coast of Espira, a location that is ideal for inter-

Precision

A piece of mimetic netting and an optical scope of good quality are the basic elements that have been used so that this Greek soldier may act as a select marksman against targets of particular importance, the bipod being very useful to stabilize the assigned rifle.

vention on the coasts and islands bathed by the Ionic, Aegean and Cretan seas. Reporting to the terrestrial Army of its country, the organization includes three battalions of infantry, of which two are always kept on an active status and the third depends on the availability of soldiers, an Artillery Battalion equipped with light pieces of 105 millimeters and an Armored squadron with medium combat tanks providing a spearhead in reconnaissance tasks and achieving success in actions that may carried out. Each of the battalions is made up of three companies of infantry and a support company, including amongst the weapons of the first are light arms such as the sub-rifles Heckler und Köck (H&K) MP5 of 9x19 millimeters Parabellum, assault rifles FAL of 7.62x51 mm (.308 Winchester) –of which a precision variant fitted with an optical sight is also used– or the medium M60 machine guns. In the Support Company are found groups of four patrols associated with wire-guided anti-tank missiles of medium range Euromissile MILAN capable of being used against

targets between 25 and 2,000 meters range, medium machine guns of 7.62 mm caliber and heavy machine guns M-2 of 12.70x99 (.50 Browning), anti-aircraft systems based on portable Stinger missiles and light mortars of 60 mm and medium of 81 mm, maintaining in reserve recoilless guns M40A1 of 106 mm installed on all-terrain Mercedes vehicles.

Their personal equipment is noted for being very complete and includes Kevlar helmets, goggles for eye-protection, tactical jackets designed to transport equipment in a very comfortable manner and a uniform in mimetic tones of green that follows the line of "tiger stripes", whilst amongst collective equipment are found tracked armored M113 vehicles capable of transporting troops in a protected mode and noted for being double mounts

for a 7.62 mm weapon and an M2 machine gun, together with combat tanks M48A5 that have been updated with an advanced direction of fire and an L7 gun of 105 mm that permits them to face other, more modern, elements.

Also within their structure must be included a unit that deals with with missions such as the reconnaissance of beaches and the destruction of submarine objects, this being a special operations element that has its base in Salamina. It is

Displacements

The M-113 armored vehicle of the United States is used by the Greeks to circulate in the area of the beachhead; thanks to its tracks this movement can be carried out without problems.

structured around groups of four commandos of type OYK, who train as combat divers, practice observation techniques at long distance and are qualified in the employment of aerial means to arrive to the areas where they must carry out their mission.

These Greek Marine infantry maintain a high level of preparation and notable motivation, qualities that give them a great capacity for action. Nevertheless the size of the space that they must cover in order to defend the maritime area that surrounds their country is an aspect that limits their effectiveness, and they center on undertaking dissuasive deployments in the islands that surround them in order to leave constancy of their willingness to repel Turkish forces, with whom they maintain old disputes, that keep them opposed, despite the fact that both are incorporated into NATO.

In their support are diverse ships of the Greek Navy that are traditionally supplied with vessels of United States origin, still maintaining in reserve some LST and LCM first launched in the years following

Combat
Medium M48A5 combat tanks noted for having been modernized and incorporating a powerful 105 millimeters gun are very useful when facing the consolidated positions of the enemy who also has heavy armaments.

the Second World War. To replace them five LST of "Jason" type displacing 4,400 tons and that can carry 300 men with their vehicles have been acquired. These vessels are complemented with a dozen LCM launches of German type 521 and fifty LCVP's, LCP,s and LCA's that it is expected will be complemented, if the negotia-

tions for their acquisition bear fruit, with up to three hovercraft of "Pomornik" class constructed in Russia or the Ukraine.

Turkish amphibious forces

The Turkish Army maintains an active Force of some four hundred thousand men that can be reinforced with another eight hundred thousand of the reserve. This impressive quantity of human resources is distributed in three divisions and 50 brigades amongst which is found a specialized amphibious Unit, as in the United States, that is known as the "Amfibi Deniz Pivade".

This Brigade, that forms part of the Turkish contribution to the defensive structure of the North Atlantic Treaty Organization, is an element made up of some 4,000 men who complete the three infantry battalions, an Artillery Battalion and the associated logistic units that sustain the deployments inherent to this force. Each Battalion is organized with a Command Company, four of Marine Infantry, one of Support and the sections of transmissions, medical and assault, elements that were used in 1974 during the Operation Atila when the Turks attacked Cyprus.

They generally participate in training with other similar forces of the Mediterranean coast or with the USM or the United States Marines, exercises that serve to reinforce their individual instruction that is of a significantly high level. The men's equipment is modern and combines Western systems with others designed in the ex Soviet Union and acquired from diverse

Anti-tank
The Turks deploy the MILAN wire-guided anti-tank missile system, a weapon that consists of a portable launcher and missiles located inside a sealed container. The range is about 1.2 miles and is capable of destroying any modern combat tank.

sources, being notable the MP5 sub-rifles, assault rifles G3 and medium MG3 machine guns fabricated locally; from abroad manufactured the RPG7 rocket launchers that fire bivalent grenades, or the portable launchers of the anti-tank system MILAN.

In order to permit deployment in any coastal area a dozen large vessels are employed that include the LST NL 125 "Osman Gazi" introduced in 1994 that can transport 900 men and 15 combat tanks, six LCT's that correspond to the French model "Edic", three LST's delivered in the 1980's that are also used for minesweeping and two units of the United States type "Terrebone Parish" constructed in the mid 1950's. The movement between ships and beaches is executed by twenty eight LCT launches that are sufficiently modern together with some twenty LCM launches.

ble of being deployed in the African provinces of Angola, Guinea Bissau and Mozambique.

Thus the "Fuzilieiros Navais" was born who carried out a tremendous labor during the confrontations in Africa, passing a total of sixty four detachments, forty six companies and 15 independent patrols, through this theatre of operations, this force being grouped into the "Commando de Fuzileiros (CCF) created under Law 275/74 of 24th June.

Today the "fuzos", as they have come to be known in their country, are some 2,500 men reporting to the Navy Chief of Staff of the Portugese Navy. Grouped together is a High Command element, the Fuerza de Fuzileiros del Continent (FFC), the Escuela de Fuzileiros (EF) and the Unidades de Fuzilieros and landing launches.

Fuzileiros Navais

The history of this force dates back to 1618 when the "Tercio de la Armada Real de la Corona de Portugal" was formed. Diverse historical events led to their dissolution and this continued until 1961, when it was recognized that it was necessary to count on a military element capa-

Specialization

The men of the "Destacamento de Operaçoes Especiais" (DAE) are a highly trained group acting as an element to signal beaches, in actions with targets of particular value, or to make up patrols of special reconnaissance.

Assault

The Greek and Turkish forces normally work together with other amphibious units of the Mediterranean coast in order to participate in multinational deployment operations that increase the capacity of NATO to respond before to any crisis in the area.

The FFC is the element of amphibious assault and has as its center of operations the Naval Base in Alfeite near Lisbon, its mission is to plan, coordinate and control the operation of the amphibious units; ensure their organization and the preparation of the Operational Forces and the Landing Force, and to exercise command over such units as are designa-

Rocket launchers
As with the rest of the Turkish Armed Forces, the "Amfibi Deniz Pivade" has been equipped with material of Russian origin amongst which are found these anti-tank launchers RPG-7 that consist of an element for aiming and grenades that are fed into the mouth at the front.

ted by the chief of the CCF.

In order that these tasks may be undertaken, an organization has been structured consisting of a command, its general staff and diverse units: the Infantry Battalion (BF1) assigned to the vigilance of the infrastructures for which the Navy is responsible and to service the ships that patrol the countries jurisdictional waters; the Infantry Battalion (BF2) that is somewhat larger than the above mentioned and better qualified to undertake amphibious missions; a unit trained to act as Naval Police; the Unit of Fire Support that uses on medium and heavy mortars, anti-aircraft weapons and anti-tank systems of short and medium range; a Tactical Transport Unit with light vehicles and several types of lorry and a Unit of Aquatic Support with several types of

"Fuzileiros"
The troops of the Portuguese Marine Infantry have their main base in Alfeite and count on two battalions specially trained to undertake the most varied of amphibious assault in support of the interests of their country and of those of NATO.

pneumatic vessels as also LARC vehicles that can navigate in water or circulate on land.

The EF has its headquarters in Vale do Zebro and its mission is to ensure the military formation –technical, physical, moral and cultural– of the students who pass through their installations, with the aim of preparing them to comply with the functions assigned to the Corps.

The level of men and support provided has permitted the making up of a Light landing Battalion of Landing that is the maximum exponent of the capacity for amphibious assault in Portugal, an element that is supported by three LCT's of "Bombarda" type capable of transporting a military load of 350 tons, and six launches of LCM 100 and LDM 400 type. Also In their support is the "Destacamento de Operaçoes Especiais"

(DAE), created in 1985, that combines a small group of men specially trained to undertake infiltration missions from submarines or helicopters, of particular note being the training and qualification as divers, the preparation to overcome every type of obstacle and their adaptation to use differents classes of weapon.

WALTHER SUB-RIFLE.

The Portuguese Navy continues to use these robust sub-rifles, manufactured since 1963 by the German company Walther to satisfy internal demand as well as the export market.

The MP-K or "Maschinenpistole" is a weapon constructed integrally of steel following a stamping process and taking as its basis an interior mechanism of recoiling mass, a design and construction conferring outstanding qualities when they are used in adverse conditions such as in marine conditions where the saltwater attacks all that which it comes into contact with.

Its basic characteristics are the firing of a 9x19 millimeter Parabellum cartridge, a weight of 3,425 kilograms when it is fed by a rectilinear magazine of 32 cartridges and its dimensions are 368 millimeters with the stock folded and 653 when extended. Its design is extremely streamlined, it does not have protuberances and is that is very reliable armament. Another outstanding feature is the ergonometric conception of the lever to select the modality of fire, semiautomatic or bursts, and the possibility of using the stock as a rest for the left hand when fired with this folded over the right side.